Party Cak

Publisher's Note: Raw or semi-cooked eggs should not be consumed by babies, toddlers, pregnant or breastfeeding women, the elderly or those suffering from a chronic illness.

Publisher & Creative Director: Nick Wells
Senior Project Editor: Catherine Taylor
Art Director: Mike Spender
Layout Design: Jane Ashley
Digital Design & Production: Chris Herbert
Proofreader: Dawn Laker

Wedding Cake, Christmas Cake and cupcakes recipes by Ann Nicol
Special thanks to Laura Bulbeck, Laura Zats, Caitlin O'Connell

This is a **FLAME TREE** Book

FLAME TREE PUBLISHING
Crabtree Hall, Crabtree Lane
Fulham, London SW6 6TY
United Kingdom
www.flametreepublishing.com

Flame Tree is part of Flame Tree Publishing Ltd

First published 2012

A copy of the CIP data for this book is available from the British Library.

Printed in China

All images © Flame Tree Publishing Ltd, except the following, which are courtesy Shutterstock and © the following suppliers: M. Unal Ozmen 14; Monkey Business Images 15; Simone van den Berg 17; Jiri Hera 18l; restyler 18r; Shawn Hempel 19; Worytko Pawel 20; Marie C Fields 21; svehlik 22.

Party Cakes

General Editor: Gina Steer

**FLAME TREE
PUBLISHING**

Contents

These dessert cakes are perfect for fancier gatherings. Whether you are inviting colleagues or friends, you are sure to impress with offerings like French Chocolate Pecan Torte or Chocolate & Saffron Cheesecake. For something a bit less traditional, perhaps try the Topsy Turvy Pudding, or indulge with Chocolate Profiteroles. There are also creamy non-chocolate options such as the Orange Fruit Cake. The simple recipes found in this section will have you baking fancy desserts like a pro!

Special Occasions 114

The best thing about festive parties is always the dessert! If you need to prepare a themed cake for a celebration, this section has the recipe you need for any occasion. There are suggestions for Christmas, Hannukah, Easter, Halloween and weddings, or indeed, you can celebrate birthdays and special events all year round – whether it's a baby shower or a house warming, Chocolate Box Cake or Rich Devil's Food Cake will go down a treat!

Tea Parties 186

These lighter cakes and cupcakes are just the thing for an afternoon tea party. Sip a nice cup of tea while enjoying Lemon Drizzle Cake or Luxury Carrot Cake. With plenty of different cupcake recipes included, such as Banoffee Cupcakes, Spring Daffodil Cupcakes and Rich Chocolate Cupcakes, you'll never run out of options for a delightful tea party at any time of the year.

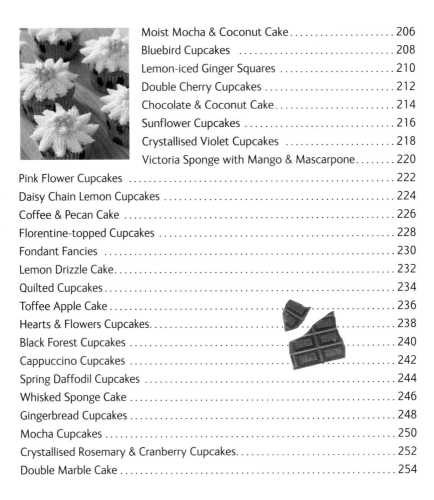

Kids' Parties. 272

Your child and their friends will be delighted with these adorable party cakes. You can find something to make a child of any age happy, from Pirate Cupcakes to Kitty Faces Cupcakes to Boys' and Girls' Names. You could even turn the baking into a family activity! Whether for a party at home or a treat to take in to school for a birthday, you and your child will love these cute cakes.

Outdoor Parties 314

On a lovely summer's day, why not go out on a picnic or have a barbecue? The cakes found here are easily cut up and popped into Tupperware to accompany you on such an occasion. The Miracle Bars and Pecan Caramel Millionaire's Shortbread are sure to be especially delicious when enjoyed after a long walk. For those really hot days, try Jammy Buns or Fruit and Nut Flapjacks for delicious snacks that won't melt onto your fingers!

Equipment & Utensils

Cooking equipment not only assists in the kitchen, but can make all the difference between success and failure. Take the humble cake tin. Although a very basic piece of cooking equipment, it plays an essential role in baking. Using a tin that is too large will spread the mixture too thinly and the result will be a flat, limp-looking cake. On the other hand, cramming the mixture into a tin which is too small will result in the mixture rising up and out of the tin.

BAKEWARE

To ensure successful baking it is worth investing in a selection of high-quality tins, which, if looked after properly, should last for many years. Follow the manufacturers' instructions when first using and ensure that the tins are thoroughly washed and dried after use and before putting away.

Sandwich Cake Tins

Perhaps the most useful of tins for baking are sandwich cake tins, ideal for classics such as Victoria

Other Tins

There are plenty of other tins to choose from, ranging from themed and shaped tins, such as Christmas trees, numbers and petals, to ring mould tins (tins with a hole in the centre) and springform tins where the sides release after cooking, allowing the finished cake to be removed easily. A selection of different-sized roasting tins is also a worthwhile investment as they can double up as a *bain-marie*, or for cooking larger quantities of cakes such as gingerbread.

OTHER ESSENTIAL ITEMS

Mixing Bowls

Three to four different sizes of mixing bowls are also very useful for mixing and melting ingredients.

Wire Cooling Racks

Another vital piece of equipment is a wire cooling

sponge cake. You will need two tins and they are normally 18 cm/7 inches or 20.5 cm/8 inches in diameter and are about 5–7.5cm/2–3 inches deep and often nonstick.

Deep Cake Tins

With deep cake tins, it is personal choice whether you buy round or square tins. They vary in size from 12.5–35.5 cm/5–14 inches with a depth of between 12.5–15 cm/5–6 inches. A deep cake tin, for everyday fruit or Madeira cake is a must, a useful size is 20.5 cm/8 inches.

Loaf Tins

Loaf tins come in two sizes: 450 g/1 lb and 900 g/2 lb.

rack. It is essential when baking to allow cakes to cool after being removed from their tins.

A wire rack also protects your kitchen surfaces from the heat and allows air to circulate around the goodies, speeding cooling and preventing soggy bottoms.

Measuring Items

Baking needs 100 per cent accuracy to ensure a perfect result. Scales come in many shapes and sizes, both digital and with weights. Most have a weigh pan although, with some, your own bowl is used. Measuring jugs and spoons are essential for accurate measuring of both your dry and wet ingredients.

Mixing Spoons and Sieves

Basic mixing cutlery is also essential, such as a wooden spoon (for mixing and creaming), a spatula (for transferring the mixture from the mixing bowl to the baking tins and spreading the mixture once it is in the tins) and a palette knife (to ease cakes out of their tins before placing them on the wire racks to cool). Also, do not forget a fine-mesh sieve, for sifting flour and powders.

ELECTRICAL EQUIPMENT

Nowadays help from time-saving gadgets and electrical equipment makes baking far easier and quicker. Equipment can be used for creaming, mixing, beating, whisking, grating and chopping. There is a wide choice of machines available, from the most basic to the highly sophisticated.

Food Processors

First decide what you need your processor to do when choosing a machine. If you are a novice to baking, it may be a waste to start with a machine which offers a wide range of implements and functions. This can be off-putting and result in not using the machine to its ultimate potential.

When buying a food processor, look for measurements on the sides of the processor bowl and machines with a removable feed tube, which allows food or liquid to be added while the motor is still running. Look out for machines that have the facility to increase the capacity of the bowl and have a pulse button for controlled chopping. For many, storage is an issue so reversible discs and flex storage, or, on more advanced models, a blade storage compartment or box, can be advantageous.

It is also worth thinking about machines which offer optional extras which can be bought as your cooking requirements change. Mini chopping bowls are available for those wanting to chop small quantities of food. If time is an issue, dishwasher-friendly attachments may be vital. Citrus presses, liquidisers and whisks may all be useful attachments for the individual cook.

Blenders

Blenders often come as attachments to food processors and are generally used for liquidising and puréeing foods. There are two main types of blender. The first is known as a goblet blender. The blades of this blender are at the bottom of the goblet with measurements up the sides. The second blender is portable. It is hand-held and should be placed in a bowl to blend.

Mixers

Table-top mixers are freestanding and are capable of dealing with fairly large quantities of mixture. They are robust machines and good for heavy cake mixing

as well as whipping cream, whisking egg whites or making one-stage cakes. These mixers also offer a wide range of attachments ranging from liquidisers to mincers, juicers, can openers and many more and varied attachments. Hand-held mixers are smaller than freestanding mixers and often come with their own bowl and stand from which they can be lifted off and used as hand-held devices. They have a motorised head with detachable twin whisks. These mixers are particularly versatile as they do not need a specific bowl in which to whisk. Any suitable mixing bowl can be used.

Essential Ingredients

The quantities may differ, but basic baking ingredients do not vary greatly. Let us take a closer look at the baking ingredients which are essential.

FAT

Butter and margarine are the fats most commonly used in baking. Others that can be used include white vegetable fat, lard and oil. Low-fat spreads are not recommended for baking, as they break down when cooked at a high temperature. Often it is a matter of personal preference which fat you choose but there are a few guidelines that are important to remember.

Butter and Margarine

Unsalted butter is the fat most commonly used in cake making, especially in rich fruit cakes and the heavier sponge cakes such as Madeira or chocolate torte. Unsalted butter gives a distinctive flavour to the cake. Some people favour margarine which imparts little or no flavour to the cake.

As a rule, butter and firm block margarine should not be used straight from the refrigerator but allowed to come to room temperature before using (allow about an hour to soften). Also, it should be beaten by itself first before creaming or rubbing in. Soft margarine is best suited to one-stage recipes.

Oil

Light oils, such as vegetable or sunflower, are sometimes used instead of solid fats. However, if oil is used, be careful – it is vital to follow a specific recipe because the proportions of oil to flour and eggs are different and these recipes will need extra raising agents.

FLOUR

We can buy a wide range of flour all designed for specific jobs. There is even a special sponge flour designed especially for whisked sponges. It is also possible to buy flours that cater for coeliacs, which contain no gluten. Buckwheat, soy and chickpea flours are also available. Flour can also come ready sifted.

Which Flour to Use

Strong flour, which is rich in gluten, whether it is white or brown (this includes granary and stoneground), is best kept for bread and Yorkshire puddings. Ordinary flour or weak flour is best for cakes, which absorbs the fat easily and gives a soft, light texture. This flour comes in plain white or self-raising, as well as wholemeal. Self-raising flour, which has the raising agent already incorporated, is best kept for sponge cakes, where it is important that an even rise is achieved.

Plain flour can be used for all types of baking. If using plain flour for cakes, unless otherwise stated in the recipe, use 1 teaspoon baking powder to 225 g/ 8 oz plain flour. With sponge cakes and light fruit cakes, it is best to use self-raising flour as the raising agent has already been added to the flour. This way there is no danger of using too much, which can result in a sunken cake with a sour taste.

Other Raising Agents

There are other raising agents that are also used. Some cakes use bicarbonate of soda with or without cream of tartar, blended with warm or sour

milk. Whisked eggs also act as a raising agent, as the air trapped in the egg ensures that the mixture rises. Generally no other raising agent is required.

EGGS

There are many types of eggs sold and it really is a question of personal preference which ones are chosen. All offer the same nutritional benefits. Store eggs in the refrigerator with the round end uppermost and allow them to come to room temperature before using.

Sizes

When a recipe states 1 egg, it is generally accepted this refers to a medium egg. Over the past few years the grading of eggs has changed. For years, eggs were sold as small, standard and large, then this method changed and they were graded in numbers with 1 being the largest. The general feeling by the public was that this system was misleading, so now we buy our eggs as small, medium and large.

Types

The majority of eggs sold in this country come from caged hens. These are the cheapest eggs and the hens have been fed on a manufactured mixed diet. Barn eggs are from hens kept in barns who are free to roam within the barn. However, their diet is similar to caged hens and the barns may be overcrowded. Free-range eggs are from hens that lead a much

more natural life and are fed natural foods. This, however, is not always the case and in some instances they may still live in a crowded environment and be fed the same foods as caged and barn hens. Organic eggs are from hens that live in a flock, whose beaks are not clipped and who are completely free to roam. Obviously, these eggs are much more expensive than the others.

Safety

Due to the slight risk of salmonella, all eggs are now sold date stamped to ensure that the eggs are used in their prime. This applies even to farm eggs which are no longer allowed to be sold straight from the farm. Look for the lion quality stamp (on 75 per cent of all eggs sold) which guarantees that the eggs come from hens vaccinated against salmonella, have been laid in the UK and are produced to the highest food safety standards. All of these eggs carry a best-before date. Do remember that raw or semi-cooked eggs should not be given to babies, toddlers, pregnant women, the elderly and those suffering from a recurring illness.

SUGAR

Sugar not only offers taste to baking but also adds texture and volume to the mixture. It is generally accepted that caster sugar is best for sponge cakes. Its fine granules disperse evenly when creaming or whisking. Granulated sugar is used for more general cooking, such as stewing fruit, whereas demerara sugar with its toffee taste and crunchy texture is good for sticky puddings and cakes. For rich fruit cakes, Christmas puddings and cakes, use the muscovado (unrefined brown) sugars, which give a rich, intense treacle flavour. Icing sugar is used primarily for icings and can be used in fruit sauces when the sugar needs to dissolve quickly.

Basic Methods

LINING

If a recipe states that the tin needs lining do not be tempted to ignore this. Rich fruit cakes and other cakes that take a long time to cook benefit from the tin being lined so that the edges and base do not burn or dry out.

Papers

Greaseproof paper or baking parchment is ideal for this. It is a good idea to have the paper at least double thickness, or preferably three to four layers. Sponge cakes and other cakes that are cooked in 30 minutes or less are also better if the bases are lined as it is far easier to remove them from the tin.

Technique

The best way to line a round or square tin is to draw lightly around the base and then cut just inside the markings, making it easy to sit in the tin. Next, lightly oil the paper so it peels easily away from the cake. If the sides of the tin also need to be lined, then cut a strip of paper long enough for the tin. This can be measured by wrapping a piece of string around the rim of the tin. Once again, lightly oil the paper, push against the tin and oil once more, as this will hold the paper to the sides of the tin.

SEPARATING EGGS

When separating eggs (that is, separating the white from the yolk), crack an egg in half lightly and cleanly over a bowl, being careful not to break the yolk and keeping it in the shell. Then tip the yolk backwards and forwards between the two shell halves, allowing as much of the white as possible to spill out into the bowl. Keep or discard the yolk and/or the white as needed. Make sure that you do

not get any yolk in your whites, as this will prevent successful whisking of the whites. It takes practice!

DIFFERENT MIXING TECHNIQUES

Rubbing In

In this method, the fat is lightly worked into the flour between the fingers, as in pastry making, until the mixture resembles fine crumbs. This can be done by hand or in a food processor. Enough liquid is stirred in to give a soft mixture that will drop easily from a spoon. This method is used for easy fruit cakes.

Creaming

The creaming method – which means that the butter and sugar are first beaten or 'creamed'

together – makes light cakes. A little care is needed for this method. Use a large mixing bowl to beat the fat and sugar together until pale and fluffy. The eggs are gradually beaten in to form a slackened batter and the flour is folded in last, to stiffen up the mixture.

All-In-One Mixtures

This 'one-stage' method is quick and easy and is perfect for those new to baking, as it does not involve any complicated techniques. It is ideal for making light sponges, but soft tub-type margarine or softened butter at room temperature must be used. All the ingredients are simply placed in a large bowl and quickly beaten together for just a few minutes until smooth. Take care not to overbeat, as this will make the mixture too wet. Self-raising flour with the addition of a little extra baking powder is vital for a good rise.

The Melting Method

Cakes with a delicious moist, sticky texture, such as gingerbread, are made by this method. These cakes use a high proportion of sugar and syrup, which are gently warmed together in a saucepan with the fat, until the sugar has dissolved and the mixture is liquid. It is important to cool the hot melted mixture a little before beating in flour, eggs and spices to make the batter, otherwise it will damage the power of the raising agent.

Icing Recipes

Beat the butter and icing sugar together until light and fluffy. Add the flavourings and colourings of choice and beat again. Add the cream cheese and whisk until light and fluffy. Do not overbeat, however, or the mixture can become runny.

BASIC BUTTERCREAM

Covers a 20 cm/8 in round cake (top) or 12 cupcakes

CREAM CHEESE FROSTING

Covers a 20 cm/8 in round cake (top) or 12 cupcakes

50 g/2 oz unsalted butter, softened
300 g/11 oz icing sugar, sifted
flavouring of choice
food colourings
125 g/4 oz cream cheese

150 g/5 oz unsalted butter, softened
225 g/8 oz icing sugar, sifted
2 tbsp hot milk or water
1 tsp vanilla extract
food colourings of choice

Beat the butter until light and fluffy, then beat in the sifted icing sugar and hot milk or water in two batches. Add the vanilla extract and any food colourings. Store chilled for up to 2 days in a lidded container.

CHOCOLATE FUDGE ICING

Covers a 20 cm/8 in round cake (top) or 12 cupcakes

125 g/4 oz dark chocolate, broken into pieces
50 g/2 oz unsalted butter
1 medium egg, beaten
175 g/6 oz natural icing sugar, sifted
$^1/_2$ tsp vanilla extract

Place the chocolate and butter in a bowl over a pan of hot water and stir until melted. Remove from the heat and beat in the egg with the icing sugar and vanilla. Beat until smooth and glossy, then use immediately, or allow to cool and thicken for a spreading consistency.

ROYAL ICING

Covers a 20 cm/8 in round cake (top) or 12 cupcakes

2 medium egg whites
500 g/1 lb 1 oz icing sugar, sifted
2 tsp lemon juice

Put the egg whites in a large bowl and whisk lightly with a fork to break up the whites until foamy. Sift in half the icing sugar with the lemon juice and beat well with an electric mixer for 4 minutes, or by hand with a wooden spoon for about 10 minutes, until smooth.

Gradually sift in the remaining icing sugar and beat again until thick, smooth and brilliant white and the icing forms soft peaks when flicked up with a spoon. Keep the royal icing covered with a clean, damp cloth until you are ready to use it, or store in the refrigerator in a tightly lidded plastic container until needed. If making royal icing ahead of time to use later, beat it again before use to remove any air bubbles that may have formed in the mixture.

GLACÉ ICING

Covers a 20 cm/8 in round cake (top) or 12 cupcakes

225 g/8 oz icing sugar
few drops lemon juice, or vanilla or almond extract
2–3 tbsp boiling water
liquid food colouring

Sift the icing sugar into a bowl and add the chosen flavouring. Gradually stir in enough water to mix to a consistency of thick cream. Beat with a wooden spoon until the icing is thick enough to coat the back of the spoon. Add colouring, if liked, and use at once because the icing will begin to form a skin.

APRICOT GLAZE

Covers two 20 cm/8 in round cakes (top) or 24 cupcakes

450 g/1 lb apricot jam
3 tbsp water
1 tsp lemon juice

Place the jam, water and juice in a heavy-based saucepan and heat gently, stirring, until soft and melted. Boil rapidly for 1 minute, then press through a fine sieve with the back of a wooden spoon. Discard the pieces of fruit. Use immediately for

glazing or sticking on almond paste and/or fondant, or pour into a clean jar or plastic container, seal and refrigerate for up to 3 months.

ALMOND PASTE

Covers two 20 cm/8 in round cakes (top) or 24 cupcakes

125 g/4 oz icing sugar, sifted
125 g/4 oz caster sugar
225 g/8 oz ground almonds
1 medium egg
1 tsp lemon juice

Stir the sugars and ground almonds together in a bowl. Whisk the egg and lemon juice together and mix into the dry ingredients.

Knead until the paste is smooth. Wrap tightly in clingfilm or foil to keep airtight and store in the refrigerator until needed. The paste can be made 2–3 days ahead of time, but after that it will start to dry out and become difficult to handle.

To use the almond paste, knead on a surface lightly dusted with icing sugar until soft and pliable. Brush the top of each cake with apricot glaze. Roll out the paste and cut out discs large enough to cover the tops of the cakes. Press onto the cakes.

SUGARPASTE

Covers a 20 cm/8 in round cake (top) or 12 cupcakes, or use for decorations

1 medium egg white
1 tbsp liquid glucose
350 g/12 oz icing sugar, sifted

Place the egg white and liquid glucose in a large mixing bowl and stir together with a fork, breaking up the egg white. Add the icing sugar gradually, mixing in with a palette knife until the mixture binds together and forms a ball. Turn the ball of sugarpaste out onto a clean surface dusted with icing sugar and knead for 5 minutes until soft but firm enough to roll out. If the icing is too soft, knead in a little more icing sugar until the mixture is pliable.

To colour, knead in paste food colouring. Do not use liquid food colour, as this is not suitable and will make the sugarpaste go limp.

To use, roll out thinly on a clean surface dusted with icing sugar and cut out discs large enough to cover the top of each cake. Brush the almond paste (if using as a layer underneath the sugarpaste discs) with a little cold boiled water or a clear spirit such as kirsch and press onto the cake, then press the sugarpaste on top of the almond paste topping. Alternatively, coat the cakes with a little buttercream, place the sugarpaste disc on top and press down.

To mould, knead lightly and roll out thinly on a surface dusted with icing sugar. Use cutters or templates to make flowers or shapes (see pages 30–31). Mould into shapes with your fingertips and leave to dry out for 24 hours in egg boxes lined with clingfilm.

Decorating

containing the chocolate is completely dry and that steam or water cannot enter the bowl. Heat the water to a gentle simmer only and leave the bowl to stand for about 5 minutes. Do not let the water get too hot or the chocolate will reach too high a temperature and will lose its sheen.

The microwave oven is ideal for melting chocolate. Place the chocolate pieces in a small microwave-proof bowl and melt gently on low or defrost settings in small bursts of 30 seconds, checking and stirring in between, until the chocolate has melted.

USING CHOCOLATE

Melting Chocolate

Care and attention are needed to melt chocolate for baking and cake decorating needs. If the chocolate gets too hot or comes into contact with water or steam, it will 'seize' or stiffen and form into a hard ball instead of a smooth melted mixture. You can add a little vegetable oil or margarine, a teaspoon at a time, to the mixture to make it liquid again. To melt chocolate, break the bar into small pieces, or grate or chop it, and place in a heatproof bowl standing over a pan of warm, not hot, water. Make sure the bowl

Making Chocolate Decorations

Curls and shavings Spread melted chocolate out thinly onto a clean dry surface such as a plastic board, marble or a clean worktop. Leave the chocolate until almost set, then pull a long, sharp-bladed knife through it at an angle to form curls or shavings. Place the curls in a lidded plastic box in the refrigerator until needed for decoration.

Leaves Wash and dry holly or rose leaves and place on a sheet of nonstick baking parchment. Melt the chocolate and paint on the underside of each leaf. Leave to dry out, then carefully peel away the leaf. You will find the veined side is uppermost on the chocolate leaf. Place in a lidded container and keep refrigerated until needed for decoration.

CRYSTALLISING PETALS, FLOWERS, LEAVES AND BERRIERS

Wash and dry herbs and leaves such as rosemary sprigs and small bay leaves or berries such as cranberries. Separate edible petals from small flowers

such as rosebuds and clean small flowers such as violets with a clean brush, but do not wash them.

Beat 1 medium egg white with 2 tsp cold water until frothy. Paint a thin layer of egg white carefully over the items, then sprinkle lightly with caster

sugar, shaking to remove any excess. Leave to dry on a wire rack lined with nonstick baking parchment.

USING BUTTERCREAM AND CREAM CHEESE FROSTINGS

These soft icings can be swirled onto the tops of cakes with a small palette knife or placed in a piping bag fitted with a star nozzle to pipe impressive whirls.

* Do not be mean with the amount of frosting you use. If this is scraped on thinly, you will see the cake underneath, so be generous.

* Keep cakes with frostings in a cool place, or refrigerate, as they contain a high percentage of butter, which will melt easily in too warm a place.

- Cakes coated in buttercream can be decorated easily with colourful sprinkles and sugars. To make this easy, place the sprinkles in a small saucer or on a piece of nonstick baking parchment and roll the outside edges of each cake in the decorations.

USING SUGARPASTE

Sugarpaste is a versatile icing, as it can be used for covering small cakes or modelling all sorts of fancy decorations. To use as a covering, roll out the sugarpaste thinly on a surface dusted with icing sugar and cut out circles the size of the cake tops. Coat each cake with a little apricot glaze or buttercream and press on the circles to form a flat surface.

Making Flat Decorations

To make letters, numbers or flat decorations, roll out the sugarpaste thinly and cut out the shapes using cutters or a sharp knife. Leave to dry on nonstick baking parchment on a flat surface or a tray for 2–3 hours to make them firm and easy to handle.

Copying Patterns from Templates

You may find a simple shape in a book or magazine that you would like to replicate in icing. Trace the pattern you want onto a sheet of clear greaseproof paper or nonstick baking parchment. Roll out the sugarpaste thinly, then position the traced pattern. Mark over the pattern with the tip of a small, sharp knife or a pin. Remove the paper and cut out the marked-on pattern with a small, sharp knife.

Making Roses

Colour the sugarpaste icing with pink paste food colouring. Take a small piece of sugarpaste and make a small cone shape, then roll a small pea-size piece of sugarpaste into a ball. Flatten out the ball into a petal shape and wrap this round the cone shape. Continue adding more petals, then trim the thick base. Leave to dry for 2 hours in a clean egg box lined with foil or clingfilm.

Making Lilies

Colour a little sugarpaste a deep yellow and mould this into thin sausage shapes. Leave these to firm on nonstick baking parchment or clingfilm for 2 hours. Thinly roll out white sugarpaste and mark out small squares of 4 x 4 cm/1½ x 1½ inches. Wrap each square round a yellow centre to form a lily and press the end together. Place the lilies on nonstick baking parchment to dry out for 2 hours.

Making Daisies

Roll out a little sugarpaste thinly and, using a daisy stamp cutter (see page 224), press out small flower shapes and mould these into a curve. Leave the daisies to dry out on nonstick baking parchment, then pipe dots into the centre of each one with yellow royal icing or a small gel tube of writing icing.

Making Butterfly Wings

Colour the sugarpaste and roll out thinly. Trace round the butterfly patterns and cut out the wing shapes. Leave these to dry flat on nonstick baking parchment for 4 hours to make them firm and easy to lift.

Decorating Tips

- Always roll out almond paste or sugarpaste icing on a surface lightly dusted with icing sugar.

- Leave sugarpaste-covered cakes to firm up for 2 hours before adding decorations, as this provides a good finished surface to work on.

- Tie ribbons round the finished cake and secure them with a dab of royal icing. Never use pins in ribbons on a cake.

- Once decorated, store sugarpaste-covered cakes in large boxes in a cool place. Do not store in a refrigerator, as the sugarpaste will become damp and colours may run.

Paste food colourings are best for working with sugarpaste and a little goes a very long way. As these are very concentrated, use a cocktail stick to add dots of paste gradually until you are sure of the colour, and knead in until even.

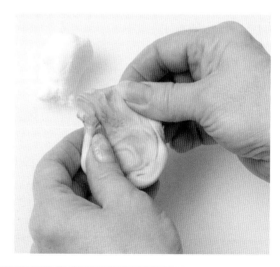

Dinner Parties

Supreme Chocolate Gateau

**CUTS INTO
10–12 SLICES**

For the cake:
175 g/6 oz self-raising
    flour, sifted
1½ tsp baking powder, sifted
3 tbsp cocoa powder, sifted

175 g/6 oz margarine or
    butter, softened
175 g/6 oz caster sugar
3 large eggs

To decorate:
350 g/12 oz dark chocolate
1 gelatine leaf
200 ml/7 fl oz double cream
75 g/3 oz butter
cocoa powder, for dusting

Preheat the oven to 180°C/350°F/Gas Mark 4, 10 minutes before baking. Lightly oil and line three 20.5 cm/8 inch round tins. Whisk all the cake ingredients together until thick; add a little warm water if very thick. Spoon into the tins. Bake for 35–40 minutes until a skewer inserted into the centre comes out clean. Cool on wire racks.

Very gently heat 2 tablespoons hot water with 50 g/2 oz of the chocolate and stir until combined. Remove from the heat and leave for 5 minutes. Place the gelatine into a dish and add 2 tablespoons cold water. Leave for 5 minutes, squeeze out any excess water and add to the chocolate. Stir until dissolved. Whip the cream until just thickened. Add the chocolate mixture and continue whisking until soft peaks form. Leave until starting to set. Place one of the cakes onto a plate and spread with half the cream mixture. Top with a second cake and the remaining cream, cover with the third cake and chill until the cream has set.

Melt 175 g/6 oz of the chocolate with the butter and stir until smooth; leave until thickened. Melt the remaining chocolate. Cut twelve 10 cm/4 inch squares of foil. Spread the chocolate evenly over them to within 2.5 cm/1 inch of the edges. Chill for 3–4 minutes until just set but not brittle. Gather up the corners and return to the refrigerator until firm. Spread the chocolate and butter mixture over the top and sides of the cake. Remove the foil from the curls and use to decorate the top of the cake. Dust with cocoa powder and serve cut into wedges.

Try this: FOR AN ALTERNATIVE: 64   FOR A TEA PARTY: 198

White Chocolate Cheesecake

**CUTS INTO
16 SLICES**

For the base:
150 g/5 oz digestive biscuits
50 g/2 oz whole almonds,
  lightly toasted
50 g/2 oz butter, melted
½ tsp almond extract

For the filling:
125 ml/4 fl oz double cream

350 g/12 oz good-quality
  white chocolate, chopped
700 g/1½ lb cream
  cheese, softened
50 g/2 oz caster sugar
4 large eggs
2 tbsp amaretto or
  almond-flavour liqueur

For the topping:
450 ml/¾ pint sour cream
50 g/2 oz caster sugar
½ tsp almond or vanilla
  extract
white chocolate curls,
  to decorate

Preheat the oven to 180°C/350°F/Gas Mark 4, 10 minutes before baking. Lightly oil a 23 x 7.5 cm/9 x 3 inch springform tin. Crush the biscuits and almonds in a food processor to form fine crumbs. Pour in the butter and almond extract and blend. Pour the crumbs into the tin and, using the back of a spoon, press onto the bottom and up the sides to within 1 cm/½ inch of the top. Bake for 5 minutes to set. Remove and transfer to a wire rack. Reduce the oven temperature to 150°C/300°F/Gas Mark 2.

Heat the cream and white chocolate in a saucepan over a low heat, stirring constantly, until melted. Remove and cool. Beat the cream cheese and sugar until smooth. Add the eggs, one at a time, beating well after each addition. Slowly beat in the cooled white chocolate cream and the amaretto and pour into the crust. Place on a baking tray and bake for 45–55 minutes until the edge of the cake is firm, but the centre is slightly soft. Reduce the temperature if the top begins to brown. Remove to a wire rack and increase the temperature to 200°C/400°F/Gas Mark 6.

Beat the sour cream, sugar and almond or vanilla extract until smooth and gently pour over the cheesecake, tilting the tin to distribute evenly. Bake for another 5 minutes. Turn off the oven and leave the door halfway open for about 1 hour. Transfer to a rack and run a sharp knife around the edge of the crust to separate from the tin. Cool and refrigerate until chilled. Remove from the tin, decorate with white chocolate curls and serve.

Try this: FOR AN ALTERNATIVE: 70 FOR A TEA PARTY: 264

Chocolate Profiteroles

SERVES 4

For the pastry:
150 ml/¼ pint water
50 g/2 oz butter
65 g/2½ oz plain flour, sifted
2 medium eggs, lightly beaten

For the custard:
300 ml/½ pint milk

pinch freshly grated nutmeg
3 medium egg yolks
50 g/2 oz caster sugar
2 tbsp plain flour, sifted
2 tbsp cornflour, sifted

For the sauce:
175 g/6 oz soft brown sugar

150 ml/¼ pint boiling water
1 tsp instant coffee granules
1 tbsp cocoa powder
1 tbsp brandy
75 g/3 oz butter
1 tbsp golden syrup

Preheat the oven to 220°C/425°F/Gas Mark 7, 15 minutes before cooking. Lightly oil two baking sheets. For the pastry, place the water and the butter in a heavy-based saucepan and bring to the boil. Remove from the heat and beat in the flour. Return to the heat and cook for 1 minute, or until the mixture forms a ball. Remove from the heat and leave to cool slightly, then gradually beat in the eggs a little at a time, beating well after each addition. Once all the eggs have been added, beat until the paste is smooth and glossy. Pipe or spoon 20 small balls onto the baking sheets, allowing plenty of room for expansion. Bake in the preheated oven for 25 minutes, or until well risen and golden brown. Reduce the oven temperature to 180°C/350°F/Gas Mark 4. Make a hole in each ball and continue to bake for a further 5 minutes. Remove from the oven and leave to cool.

For the custard, place the milk and nutmeg in a heavy-based saucepan and bring to the boil. In another pan, whisk together the yolks, sugar and the flours, then beat in the hot milk. Bring to the boil and simmer, whisking constantly, for 2 minutes. Cover and leave to cool. Spoon the custard into the profiteroles and arrange on a large serving dish. Place all the sauce ingredients in a small saucepan and bring to the boil, then simmer for 10 minutes. Remove from the heat and cool slightly before serving with the profiteroles.

Try this: FOR AN ALTERNATIVE: 62   FOR A TEA PARTY: 190

White Chocolate & Passion Fruit Cake

SERVES 8–10

125 g/4 oz white chocolate
125 g/4 oz butter
225 g/8 oz caster sugar
2 medium eggs
125 ml/4 fl oz sour cream
200 g/7 oz plain
   flour, sifted

75 g/3 oz self-raising
   flour, sifted
125 g/4 oz white chocolate,
   coarsely grated,
   to decorate

For the icing:
200 g/7 oz caster sugar
4 tbsp passion fruit juice
   (about 8–10 passion
   fruit, sieved)
1½ tbsp passion fruit seeds
250 g/9 oz unsalted butter

Preheat the oven to 180°C/350°F/Gas Mark 4, 10 minutes before baking. Lightly oil and line two 20.5 cm/8 inch cake tins. Melt the white chocolate, stir in 125 ml/4 fl oz warm water and stir, then leave to cool. Whisk the butter and sugar together until light and fluffy, then add the eggs, one at a time, beating well after each addition. Beat in the chocolate mixture, sour cream and sifted flours. Divide the mixture into eight portions. Spread one portion into each of the tins. Bake in the oven for 10 minutes, or until firm, then turn out onto wire racks. Repeat with the remaining mixture to make eight cake layers.

For the icing, place 125 ml/4 fl oz water with 50 g/2 oz of the sugar in a saucepan. Heat gently, stirring, until the sugar has dissolved. Bring to the boil and simmer for 2 minutes. Remove from the heat, cool, then add 2 tablespoons of the passion fruit juice. Reserve. Blend the remaining sugar with 50 ml/2 fl oz water in a saucepan and stir constantly over a low heat, without boiling, until the sugar has dissolved. Remove from the heat and cool. Stir in the remaining juice and the seeds. Cool, then strain. Using an electric whisk, beat the butter in a bowl until very pale. Gradually beat in the syrup.

Place one layer of cake on a serving plate. Brush with the syrup and spread with a thin layer of icing. Repeat with the remaining cake, syrup and icing. Cover the cake with the remaining icing. Press the grated chocolate into the top and sides to decorate.

Try this: FOR AN ALTERNATIVE: 94 FOR A TEA PARTY: 196

Sauternes & Olive Oil Cake

SERVES 8–10

125 g/4 oz plain flour
4 medium eggs
125 g/4 oz caster sugar
grated zest of ½ lemon
grated zest of ½ orange

2 tbsp Sauternes or other
   sweet dessert wine
3 tbsp very best-quality
   extra virgin olive oil
4 ripe peaches

1–2 tsp soft brown sugar, or
   to taste
1 tbsp lemon juice
icing sugar, for dusting

Preheat the oven to 140°C/275°F/Gas Mark 1. Oil and line a 25.5 cm/10 inch springform tin. Sift the flour onto a large sheet of greaseproof paper and reserve. Using a freestanding electric mixer, if possible, whisk the eggs and sugar together until pale and stiff. Add the lemon and orange zests.

Turn the speed to low and pour the flour from the paper in a slow, steady stream onto the eggs and sugar mixture. Immediately add the wine and olive oil and switch the machine off, as the olive oil should not be incorporated completely.

Using a rubber spatula, fold the mixture very gently three or four times so that the ingredients are just incorporated. Pour the mixture immediately into the prepared tin and bake in the preheated oven for 20–25 minutes, without opening the door for at least 15 minutes. Test if cooked by pressing the top lightly with a clean finger – if it springs back, remove from the oven, if not, bake for a little longer.

Leave the cake to cool in the tin on a wire rack. Remove the cake from the tin when cool enough to handle. Meanwhile, skin the peaches and cut into segments. Toss with the brown sugar and lemon juice and reserve. When the cake is cold, dust generously with icing sugar, cut into wedges and serve with the peaches.

Try this: FOR AN ALTERNATIVE: 98   FOR A TEA PARTY: 220

Chocolate Walnut Squares

MAKES 24

125 g/4 oz butter
150 g/5 oz dark chocolate, broken into squares
450 g/1 lb caster sugar
½ tsp vanilla extract
200 g/7 oz plain flour

75 g/3 oz self-raising flour
50 g/2 oz cocoa powder
225 g/8 oz mayonnaise, at room temperature

For the chocolate glaze:
125 g/4 oz dark chocolate, broken into squares
40 g/1½ oz unsalted butter
24 walnut halves
1 tbsp icing sugar, for dusting

Preheat the oven to 170°C/325°F/Gas Mark 3, 10 minutes before baking. Oil and line a 28 x 18 x 5 cm/11 x 7 x 2 inch cake tin with nonstick baking parchment. Place the butter, chocolate, sugar, vanilla extract and 225 ml/8 fl oz cold water in a heavy-based saucepan. Heat gently, stirring occasionally, until the chocolate and butter have melted, but do not allow to boil.

Sift the flours and cocoa powder into a large bowl and make a well in the centre. Add the mayonnaise and about one third of the chocolate mixture and beat until smooth. Gradually beat in the remaining chocolate mixture. Pour into the tin and bake on the centre shelf of the oven for 1 hour, or until slightly risen and firm to the touch. Place the tin on a wire rack and leave to cool. Remove the cake and peel off the baking parchment.

For the chocolate glaze, place the chocolate and butter in a small saucepan with 1 tablespoon water and heat very gently, stirring occasionally, until melted and smooth. Leave to cool until the chocolate has thickened, then spread evenly over the cake. Chill the cake in the refrigerator for about 5 minutes, then mark into 24 squares.

Lightly dust the walnut halves with a little icing sugar and place one on the top of each square. Cut into pieces and store in an airtight container until ready to serve.

Try this: FOR AN ALTERNATIVE: 90 FOR A TEA PARTY: 226

Chocolate & Saffron Cheesecake

SERVES 6

¼ tsp saffron threads
175 g/6 oz plain flour
pinch salt
75 g/3 oz butter
1 tbsp caster sugar
1 medium egg yolk

350 g/12 oz curd cheese
75 g/3 oz golden
   granulated sugar
125 g/4 oz dark chocolate,
   melted
   and cooled

6 tbsp milk
3 medium eggs
1 tbsp icing sugar, sifted,
   to decorate

Preheat the oven to 200°C/400°F/Gas Mark 6, 15 minutes before baking. Lightly oil a 20.5 cm/ 8 inch fluted flan tin. Soak the saffron threads in 1 tablespoon hot water for 20 minutes. Sift the flour and salt into a bowl. Cut the butter into small dice, then add to the flour and, using your fingertips, rub in the butter until the mixture resembles breadcrumbs. Stir in the sugar.

Beat the egg yolk with 1 tablespoon cold water, add to the mixture and mix together until a smooth and pliable dough is formed. Add a little extra water if necessary. Knead on a lightly floured surface until free from cracks, then wrap in clingfilm and chill in the refrigerator for 30 minutes, then roll the pastry out on a lightly floured surface and use to line the tin. Prick the pastry base and sides with a fork and line with nonstick baking parchment and baking beans. Bake blind in the oven for 12 minutes. Remove the beans and parchment and continue to bake blind for 5 minutes.

Beat together the curd cheese and granulated sugar, then beat in the melted chocolate, saffron liquid, milk and eggs. Mix until blended thoroughly. Pour the mixture into the cooked flan case and place on a baking sheet. Reduce the oven temperature to 190°C/375°F/Gas Mark 5 and bake for 15 minutes, then reduce the oven temperature again to 180°C/350°F/Gas Mark 4 and continue to bake for 20–30 minutes until set. Remove the cheesecake from the oven and leave for 10 minutes before removing from the flan tin, if serving warm. If serving cold, leave in the flan tin to cool before removing and placing on a serving platter. Sprinkle with icing sugar before serving.

Try this: FOR AN ALTERNATIVE: 62   FOR A TEA PARTY: 194

Sachertorte

SERVES 10–12

150 g/5 oz dark chocolate
150 g/5 oz unsalted
butter, softened
125 g/4 oz caster sugar,
plus 2 tbsp

3 medium eggs, separated
150 g/5 oz plain flour, sifted

To decorate:
225 g/8 oz apricot jam

125 g/4 oz dark chocolate,
chopped
125 g/4 oz unsalted butter
25 g/1 oz milk chocolate

Preheat the oven to 180°C/350°F/Gas Mark 4, 10 minutes before baking. Lightly oil and line a deep 23 cm/9 inch cake tin. Melt the chocolate in a heatproof bowl set over a saucepan of simmering water. Stir in 1 tablespoon water; leave to cool.

Beat the butter and 125 g/4 oz of the sugar together until light and fluffy. Beat in the egg yolks, one at a time, beating well after each addition. Stir in the melted chocolate, then the flour. In a clean, grease-free bowl, whisk the egg whites until stiff peaks form, then whisk in the remaining sugar. Fold into the chocolate mixture and spoon into the tin. Bake in the oven for 30 minutes until firm. Leave for 5 minutes, then turn out onto a wire rack to cool. Leave the cake upside down.

To decorate, split the cake in two and place one half on a plate. Heat the jam and rub through a fine sieve. Brush half the jam onto the first cake half, then cover with the remaining half and brush with the remaining jam. Leave at room temperature for 1 hour, or until the jam has set. Place the dark chocolate with the butter into a heatproof bowl set over a saucepan of simmering water and heat until the chocolate has melted. Stir occasionally until smooth, then leave until thickened. Use to cover the cake. Melt the milk chocolate in a heatproof bowl set over a saucepan of simmering water. Place in a small, greaseproof piping bag and snip a small hole at the tip. Pipe 'Sacher' with a large 'S' on the top. Leave to set at room temperature.

Try this: FOR AN ALTERNATIVE: 76 FOR A TEA PARTY: 270

Rich Chocolate & Orange Mousse Dessert

SERVES 8

8–12 sponge finger biscuits	40 g/1½ oz cocoa	1 orange, thinly sliced
225 g/8 oz dark chocolate,	powder, sifted	300 ml/½ pint double cream
broken into pieces	125 g/4 oz icing sugar, sifted	
225 g/8 oz unsalted butter	5 medium eggs, separated	
2 tbsp orange flower water	50 g/2 oz caster sugar	

Oil and line a 900 g/2 lb loaf tin with clingfilm, taking care to keep the clingfilm as wrinkle free as possible. Arrange the sponge finger biscuits around the edge of the loaf tin, trimming the biscuits to fit if necessary. Place the chocolate, butter and orange flower water in a heavy-based saucepan and heat gently, stirring occasionally, until the chocolate has melted and is smooth. Remove the saucepan from the heat, add the cocoa powder and 50 g/2 oz of the icing sugar. Stir until smooth, then beat in the egg yolks.

In a clean, grease-free bowl, whisk the egg whites until stiff but not dry. Sift in the remaining icing sugar and whisk until stiff and glossy. Fold the egg white mixture into the chocolate mixture and, using a metal spoon or rubber spatula, stir until well blended. Spoon the mousse mixture into the loaf tin and level the surface. Cover and chill in the refrigerator until set.

Place the caster sugar with 150 ml/¼ pint water in a heavy-based saucepan and heat until the sugar has dissolved. Bring to the boil and boil for 5 minutes. Add the orange slices and simmer for about 2–4 minutes until the slices become opaque. Drain on absorbent kitchen paper; reserve.

Trim the top of the biscuits to the same level as the mousse. Invert onto a plate and remove the tin and clingfilm. Whip the cream until soft peaks form and spoon into a piping bag fitted with a star nozzle. Pipe swirls on top of the mousse and decorate with the orange slices. Chill in the refrigerator before serving.

Try this: FOR AN ALTERNATIVE: 104 FOR A TEA PARTY: 194

Marzipan Cake

SERVES 12–14

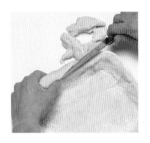

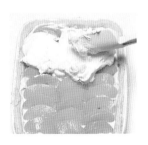

450 g/1 lb blanched almonds
300 g/11 oz icing sugar
(includes sugar for
dusting and rolling)
4 medium egg whites
125 g/4 oz Madeira cake

2 tbsp Marsala wine
225 g/8 oz ricotta cheese
50 g/2 oz caster sugar
grated zest of 1 lemon
50 g/2 oz candied peel,
finely chopped

25 g/1 oz glacé cherries,
finely chopped
425 g can peach halves,
drained
200 ml/⅓ pint double cream

Grind the blanched almonds in a food processor until fairly fine. Mix with 200 g/7 oz of the icing sugar. Beat the egg whites until stiff, then fold into the almond mixture using a metal spoon or rubber spatula to form a stiffish dough. It will still be quite sticky but will firm up as it rests. Leave for 30 minutes.

Dust a work surface very generously with some of the remaining icing sugar so that the marzipan does not stick. Roll out two thirds of the marzipan into a large sheet to a thickness of about 5 mm/¼ inch. Use to line a sloping-sided baking dish with a base measuring 25.5 cm x 20.5 cm/10 x 8 inches. Trim the edges and put any trimmings with the remainder of the marzipan.

Cut the Madeira cake into thin slices and make a layer of sponge to cover the bottom of the marzipan. Sprinkle with the Marsala wine. Beat the ricotta with the sugar and add the lemon zest, candied peel and cherries. Spread this over the sponge. Slice the peaches and put them on top of the ricotta. Whip the cream and spread it over the peaches. Roll out the remaining marzipan and lay it over the cream to seal the whole cake, pressing down gently to remove any air. Press the edges of the marzipan together. Chill in the refrigerator for 2 hours.

Turn the cake out onto a serving plate and dust generously with icing sugar. Slice thickly and serve immediately.

Try this: FOR AN ALTERNATIVE: 106   FOR A TEA PARTY: 220

Indulgent Chocolate Squares

SERVES 16

350 g/12 oz dark chocolate
175 g/6 oz butter, softened
175 g/6 oz soft light
   brown sugar
175 g/6 oz ground almonds
6 large eggs, separated

3 tbsp cocoa powder, sifted
75 g/3 oz fresh brown
   breadcrumbs
125 ml/4 fl oz double cream
50 g/2 oz white chocolate,
   chopped

50 g/2 oz milk chocolate,
   chopped
few freshly sliced
   strawberries,
   to decorate

Preheat the oven to 180°C/350°F/Gas Mark 4, 10 minutes before baking. Oil and line a deep 20.5 cm/8 inch square cake tin with nonstick baking parchment. Melt 225 g/8 oz of the dark chocolate in a heatproof bowl set over a saucepan of almost boiling water. Stir until smooth, then leave until just cool, but not beginning to set.

Beat the butter and sugar together until light and fluffy. Stir in the melted chocolate, ground almonds, egg yolks, cocoa powder and breadcrumbs. Whisk the egg whites until stiff peaks form, then stir a large spoonful into the chocolate mixture. Gently fold in the rest, then pour the mixture into the prepared tin.

Bake on the centre shelf in the preheated oven for 1¼ hours, or until firm, covering the top with foil after 45 minutes to prevent it over-browning. Leave in the tin for 20 minutes, then turn out onto a wire rack and leave to cool.

Melt the remaining 125 g/4 oz plain chocolate with the cream in a heatproof bowl set over a saucepan of almost boiling water, stirring occasionally. Leave to cool for 20 minutes, or until thickened slightly.

Spread the topping over the cake. Scatter over the white and milk chocolate and leave to set. Cut into 16 squares and serve decorated with a few freshly sliced strawberries, then serve.

Try this: FOR AN ALTERNATIVE: 84   FOR A TEA PARTY: 202

Almond Angel Cake with Amaretto Cream

**CUTS INTO
10–12 SLICES**

175 g/6 oz icing sugar, plus
2–3 tbsp
150 g/5 oz plain flour
350 ml/12 fl oz egg whites
(about 10 large egg whites)

1½ tsp cream of tartar
½ tsp vanilla extract
1 tsp almond extract
¼ tsp salt
200 g/7 oz caster sugar

175 ml/6 fl oz double cream
2 tbsp amaretto liqueur
fresh raspberries, to
decorate

Preheat the oven to 180°C/350°F/Gas Mark 4, 10 minutes before baking. Sift together the 175 g/6 oz icing sugar and the flour. Stir to blend, then sift again and reserve. Using an electric whisk, beat the egg whites, cream of tartar, vanilla extract, ½ teaspoon of the almond extract and the salt on medium speed until soft peaks form. Gradually add the caster sugar, 2 tablespoons at a time, beating well after each addition, until stiff peaks form.

Sift about one third of the flour mixture over the egg white mixture and gently fold in. Repeat, folding the flour mixture into the egg white mixture in two more batches. Spoon gently into an ungreased angel food cake tin or 25.5 cm/10 inch tube tin. Bake in the oven until risen and golden on top and the surface springs back quickly when gently pressed with a clean finger. Immediately invert the cake tin and cool completely in the tin.

When cool, carefully run a sharp knife around the edge of the tin and the centre ring to loosen the cake from the edge. Using the fingertips, ease the cake from the tin and invert onto a cake plate. Thickly dust the cake with the extra icing sugar. Whip the cream with the remaining almond extract, the liqueur and a little more icing sugar until soft peaks form. Fill a piping bag fitted with a star nozzle with half the cream and pipe around the bottom edge of the cake. Decorate the edge with the fresh raspberries and serve the remaining cream separately.

Try this: FOR AN ALTERNATIVE: 52   FOR A TEA PARTY: 258

White Chocolate Eclairs

SERVES 4–6

50 g/2 oz unsalted butter
65 g/2½ oz plain flour, sifted
2 medium eggs, lightly
    beaten
6 ripe passion fruit

300 ml/½ pint double cream
3 tbsp kirsch
1 tbsp icing sugar
125 g/4 oz white chocolate,
    broken into pieces

Preheat the oven to 190°C/375°F/Gas Mark 5, 10 minutes before baking. Lightly oil a baking sheet. Place the butter and 150 ml/¼ pint water in a saucepan and heat until the butter has melted, then bring to the boil. Remove from the heat and immediately add the flour all at once, beating with a wooden spoon until the mixture forms a ball. Leave to cool for 3 minutes. Add the eggs a little at a time, beating well after each addition, until the paste is smooth, shiny and of a piping consistency.

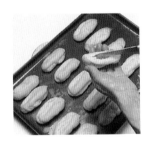

Spoon the mixture into a piping bag fitted with a plain nozzle. Sprinkle the oiled baking sheet with water. Pipe the mixture onto the baking sheet in 7.5 cm/3 inch lengths, using a knife to cut each pastry length neatly. Bake in the preheated oven for 18–20 minutes until well risen and golden. Make a slit along the side of each eclair to let the steam escape. Return the eclairs to the oven for a further 2 minutes to dry out. Transfer to a wire rack and leave to cool.

Halve the passion fruit and, using a small spoon, scoop the pulp of 4 of the fruits into a bowl. Add the cream, kirsch and icing sugar and whip until the cream holds its shape. Carefully spoon or pipe into the eclairs. Melt the chocolate in a small, heatproof bowl set over a saucepan of simmering water and stir until smooth. Leave to cool slightly, then spread over the tops of the eclairs. Scoop the pulp out of the remaining fruits. Sieve. Drizzle the juice around the eclairs and serve.

Try this: FOR AN ALTERNATIVE: 40 FOR A TEA PARTY: 234

Triple Chocolate Cheesecake

SERVES 6

For the base:
150 g/5 oz digestive biscuits, crushed
50 g/2 oz butter, melted

For the cheesecake:
75 g/3 oz white chocolate, roughly chopped

300 ml/½ pint double cream
50 g/2 oz caster sugar
3 medium eggs, beaten
400 g/14 oz full-fat soft cream cheese
2 tbsp cornflour
75 g/3 oz dark chocolate, roughly chopped

75 g/3 oz milk chocolate, roughly chopped
fromage frais, to serve

Preheat the oven to 180°C/350°F/Gas Mark 4, 10 minutes before baking. Lightly oil a 23 x 7.5 cm/9 x 3 inch springform tin.

To make the base, mix together the crushed biscuits and melted butter. Press into the base of the tin and leave to set. Chill in the refrigerator.

Place the white chocolate and cream in a small, heavy-based saucepan and heat gently until the chocolate has melted. Stir until smooth and reserve.

Beat the sugar and eggs together until light and creamy in colour, add the cream cheese and beat until the mixture is smooth and free from lumps. Stir the reserved white chocolate cream together with the cornflour into the soft cream cheese mixture. Add the dark and milk chocolate to the soft cream cheese mixture and mix lightly together until blended. Spoon over the chilled base, place on a baking sheet and bake in the oven for 1 hour.

Switch off the heat, open the oven door and leave the cheesecake to cool in the oven. Chill in the refrigerator for at least 6 hours before removing the cheesecake from the tin. Cut into slices and transfer to serving plates. Serve with fromage frais.

Try this: FOR AN ALTERNATIVE: 36   FOR A TEA PARTY: 254

Chocolaty Puffs

MAKES 12

For the choux pastry:
150 g/5 oz plain flour
2 tbsp cocoa powder
½ tsp salt
1 tbsp granulated sugar
125 g/4 oz butter, cut
  into pieces
5 large eggs

For the chocolate
  cream filling:
225 g/8 oz dark chocolate,
  chopped
600 ml/1 pint double cream
1 tbsp caster sugar (optional)
2 tbsp crème de cacao
  (optional)

For the chocolate sauce:
225 g/8 oz dark chocolate
300 ml/½ pint whipping
  cream
50 g/2 oz butter, diced
1–2 tbsp golden syrup
1 tsp vanilla extract

Preheat the oven to 220°C/425°F/Gas Mark 7, 15 minutes before baking. Lightly oil a large baking sheet. To make the choux pastry, sift the flour and cocoa powder together. Place 250 ml/ 8 fl oz water, the salt, sugar and butter in a saucepan and bring to the boil. Remove from the heat and add the flour mixture, beating vigorously with a wooden spoon until the mixture forms a ball. Return to the heat and cook for 1 minute, stirring, then cool slightly. Using an electric mixer, beat in 4 of the eggs, one at a time, beating well after each addition. Beat the last egg and add a little at a time until the dough is thick and shiny and just falls from a spoon when tapped lightly on the side of the saucepan. Pipe or spoon 12 large puffs onto the baking sheet, leaving space between. Bake for 30–35 minutes until puffy and golden. Remove from the oven, slice off the top third of each bun and return to the oven for 5 minutes to dry out. Remove and leave to cool.

For the filling, heat the chocolate with 125 ml/4 fl oz of the double cream and the caster sugar, if using, stirring until smooth, then leave to cool. Whisk the remaining cream until soft peaks form and stir in the crème de cacao, if using. Quickly fold the cream into the chocolate, then spoon or pipe into the choux buns and place the lids on top.

Place the sauce ingredients in a small saucepan and heat gently, stirring until smooth. Remove from the heat and leave to cool, stirring occasionally, until thickened. Pour over the puffs and serve.

Try this: FOR AN ALTERNATIVE: 38 FOR A TEA PARTY: 190

Black Forest Gateau

**CUTS INTO
10–12 SLICES**

250 g/9 oz butter
1 tbsp instant coffee
  granules
350 ml/12 fl oz hot water
200 g/7 oz dark chocolate,
  chopped or broken

400 g/14 oz caster sugar
225 g/8 oz self-raising flour
150 g/5 oz plain flour
50 g/2 oz cocoa powder
2 medium eggs
2 tsp vanilla extract

2 x 400 g cans stoned
  cherries in juice
2 tsp arrowroot
600 ml/1 pint double cream
50 ml/2 fl oz kirsch

Preheat the oven to 150˚C/300˚F/Gas Mark 2, 5 minutes before baking. Lightly oil and line a deep 23 cm/9 inch cake tin. Melt the butter in a large saucepan. Blend the coffee with the hot water, add to the butter with the chocolate and sugar and heat gently, stirring until smooth. Pour into a bowl and leave until just warm. Sift together the flours and cocoa powder. Using an electric mixer, whisk the chocolate mixture on a low speed, then gradually whisk in the dry ingredients. Whisk in the eggs one at a time, then the vanilla extract. Pour the mixture into the tin and bake in the preheated oven for 1¾ hours, or until firm and a skewer inserted into the centre comes out clean. Leave in the tin for 5 minutes to cool slightly before turning out onto a wire rack.

Place the cherries and their juice in a small saucepan and heat gently. Blend the arrowroot with 2 teaspoons water until smooth, then stir into the cherries. Cook, stirring, until the liquid thickens. Simmer very gently for 2 minutes, then leave until cold.

Whisk the double cream until thick. Trim the top of the cake if necessary, then split the cake into three layers. Brush the base of the cake with half the kirsch. Top with a layer of cream and one third of the cherries. Repeat the layering, then place the third layer on top. Reserve a little cream for decorating and use the remainder to cover the top and sides of the cake. Pipe a decorative edge around the cake, then arrange the remaining cherries in the centre and serve.

Chocolate Raspberry Mille Feuille

SERVES 6

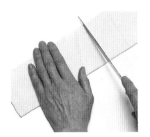

450 g/1 lb puff pastry, thawed if frozen
400 ml/14 fl oz whipping cream
275 g/10 oz seedless raspberry jam

225 g/8 oz dark chocolate, chopped
700 g/1½ lb fresh raspberries, plus extra for decorating
icing sugar, for dusting

For the raspberry sauce:
225 g/8 oz fresh raspberries
2 tbsp seedless raspberry jam
1–2 tbsp caster sugar
2 tbsp lemon juice or framboise liqueur

Preheat the oven to 200°C/400°F/Gas Mark 6, 15 minutes before baking. Lightly oil a large baking sheet and sprinkle with a little water. Roll out the pastry on a lightly floured surface to a rectangle about 43 x 28 cm/17 x 11 inches. Cut into three long strips. Using a sharp knife, mark each strip crossways at 6.5 cm/2½ inch intervals. Carefully transfer to the baking sheet, keeping the edges as straight as possible. Bake for 20 minutes, or until well risen and golden brown. Place on a wire rack and leave to cool. Carefully transfer each rectangle to a work surface and, using a sharp knife, trim the long edges straight. Cut along the knife marks to make 18 rectangles.

Make raspberry chocolate ganache by placing the cream and jam in a saucepan and bring to the boil, whisking constantly to dissolve the jam. Remove from the heat and add the chocolate all at once, stirring until the chocolate has melted. Chill. Place all the raspberry sauce ingredients in a food processor and blend until smooth. If the purée is too thick, add a little water. Adjust the sweetness if necessary. Strain into a bowl, cover and chill.

Place one rectangle on the work surface, flat-side down, spread with a little ganache and sprinkle with a few raspberries. Spread a second rectangle with ganache, place over the first, pressing gently, then sprinkle with raspberries. Place a third rectangle on top, flat-side up, and spread with ganache. Arrange some raspberries on top and dust lightly with a little icing sugar. Repeat with the remaining pastry rectangles, chocolate ganache and fresh raspberries. Chill in the refrigerator until required and serve with the raspberry sauce and any remaining fresh raspberries.

Try this: FOR AN ALTERNATIVE: 102   FOR A TEA PARTY: 196

Apple & Cinnamon Crumble–top Cake

CUTS INTO 8 SLICES

For the topping:
350 g/12 oz eating apples, peeled
1 tbsp lemon juice
125 g/4 oz self-raising flour
1 tsp ground cinnamon
75 g/3 oz butter or margarine

75 g/3 oz demerara sugar
1 tbsp milk

For the base:
125 g/4 oz butter or margarine
125 g/4 oz caster sugar
2 medium eggs

150 g/5 oz self-raising flour
cream or freshly made custard, to serve

Preheat the oven to 180°C/350°F/Gas Mark 4, 10 minutes before baking. Lightly oil and line the base of a 20.5 cm/8 inch, deep, round cake tin with greaseproof paper or baking parchment.

Finely chop the apples and mix with the lemon juice. Reserve while making the cake.

For the crumble topping, sift the flour and cinnamon together into a large bowl. Rub the butter or margarine into the flour and cinnamon until the mixture resembles coarse breadcrumbs. Stir the sugar into the breadcrumbs and reserve.

For the base, cream the butter or margarine and sugar together until light and fluffy. Gradually beat the eggs into the sugar and butter mixture a little at a time until all the egg has been added. Sift the flour and gently fold in with a metal spoon or rubber spatula.

Spoon into the base of the prepared cake tin. Arrange the apple pieces on top, then lightly stir the milk into the crumble mixture.

Scatter the crumble mixture over the apples and bake in the preheated oven for 1½ hours. Serve cold with cream or custard.

Try this: FOR AN ALTERNATIVE: 110   FOR A TEA PARTY: 236

Orange Chocolate Cheesecake

SERVES 8

225 g/8 oz plain digestive biscuits
50 g/2 oz butter
450 g/1 lb mixed fruits, such as blueberries and raspberries

1 tbsp icing sugar, sifted
few fresh mint sprigs, to decorate

For the filling:
450 g/1 lb soft cream cheese

11 g packet gelatine
350 g/12 oz orange chocolate, broken into segments
600 ml/1 pint double cream

Lightly oil and line a 20.5 cm/8 inch round, loose-bottomed, cake tin with nonstick baking parchment. Place the biscuits in a polythene bag and crush using a rolling pin. Alternatively, use a food processor. Melt the butter in a medium-sized, heavy-based saucepan, add the crushed biscuits and mix well. Press the biscuit mixture into the base of the lined tin, then chill in the refrigerator for 20 minutes.

For the filling, remove the cream cheese from the refrigerator at least 20 minutes before using, to allow the cheese to come to room temperature. Place the cream cheese in a bowl and beat until smooth, and reserve.

Pour 4 tablespoons water into a small bowl and sprinkle over the gelatine. Leave to stand for 5 minutes until spongy. Place the bowl over a saucepan of simmering water and allow to dissolve, stirring occasionally. Leave to cool slightly.

Melt the orange chocolate in a heatproof bowl set over a saucepan of simmering water, then leave to cool slightly. Whip the cream until soft peaks form. Fold the gelatine and chocolate into the cream cheese. Loosely fold in the cream, in order to create a marbled effect. Spoon into the tin and level the surface. Chill in the refrigerator for 4 hours until set. Remove the cheesecake from the tin and place on a serving plate. Top with the fruits, dust with icing sugar and decorate with sprigs of mint.

Try this: FOR AN ALTERNATIVE: 108 FOR A TEA PARTY: 232

Topsy Turvy Pudding

SERVES 6

For the topping:
175 g/6 oz demerara sugar
2 oranges

For the sponge:
175 g/6 oz butter, softened

175 g/6 oz caster sugar
3 medium eggs, beaten
175 g/6 oz self-raising
    flour, sifted
50 g/2 oz dark chocolate,
    melted

grated zest of 1 orange
25 g/1 oz cocoa powder,
    sifted
custard or sour cream,
    to serve

Preheat the oven to 180°C/350°F/Gas Mark 4, 10 minutes before baking. Lightly oil a 20.5 cm/8 inch, deep, round, loose-bottomed cake tin. Place the demerara sugar and 3 tablespoons water in a small, heavy-based saucepan and heat gently until the sugar has dissolved. Swirl the saucepan or stir with a clean wooden spoon to ensure the sugar has dissolved, then bring to the boil and boil rapidly until a golden caramel is formed. Pour into the bottom of the tin and leave to cool.

For the sponge, cream the butter and sugar together until light and fluffy. Gradually beat in the eggs a little at a time, beating well after each addition. Add a spoonful of flour after each addition to prevent the mixture curdling. Add the melted chocolate and then stir well. Fold in the orange zest, self-raising flour and sifted cocoa powder and mix well.

Remove the peel from both oranges, taking care to remove as much of the pith as possible. Thinly slice the peel into strips and then slice the oranges. Arrange the peel and then the orange slices over the caramel. Top with the sponge mixture and level the top. Place the tin on a baking sheet and bake in the preheated oven for 40–45 minutes until well risen, golden brown and an inserted skewer comes out clean. Remove from the oven, leave for about 5 minutes, invert onto a serving plate and sprinkle with cocoa powder. Serve with either custard or sour cream.

Try this: FOR AN ALTERNATIVE: 92   FOR A TEA PARTY: 266

Hazelnut, Chocolate & Chestnut Meringue Torte

SERVES 8–10

For the chocolate meringue:
1 medium egg white
50 g/2 oz caster sugar
2 tbsp cocoa powder

For the hazelnut meringue:
75 g/3 oz hazelnuts, toasted

2 medium egg whites
125 g/4 oz caster sugar

For the filling:
300 ml/½ pint double cream
250 g can sweetened
    chestnut purée

50 g/2 oz dark chocolate,
    melted
25 g/1 oz dark chocolate,
    grated

Preheat the oven to 130°C/250°F/Gas Mark ½. Line three baking sheets with baking parchment and draw a 20.5 cm/8 inch circle on each. Beat 1 egg white until stiff peaks form. Beat in 25 g/1 oz of the sugar until shiny. Mix the cocoa powder with the remaining 25 g/1 oz sugar and add 1 tablespoon at a time, beating well after each addition, until all the sugar is added and the mixture is stiff and glossy. Spread onto one of the baking sheets within the circle on the underside. Put the hazelnuts in a food processor and blend until chopped. In a clean bowl, beat the 2 egg whites until stiff. Add 50 g/2 oz of the sugar and beat. Add the remaining sugar about 1 tablespoon at a time, beating after each addition, until all the sugar is added and the mixture is stiff and glossy. Reserve 2 tablespoons of the nuts, then fold in the remainder and divide between the two remaining baking sheets. Sprinkle one of the hazelnut meringues with the reserved hazelnuts and transfer all the baking sheets to the oven. Bake for 1½ hours. Turn the oven off and leave there until cold.

Whip the cream until thick. Beat the purée in another bowl until soft. Fold in a spoonful of the cream, then add the remaining cream and the melted chocolate and fold together. Place the plain hazelnut meringue on a serving plate. Top with half the cream and chestnut mixture. Add the chocolate meringue and top with the remaining cream. Add the final meringue. Sprinkle over the grated chocolate and serve.

Try this: FOR AN ALTERNATIVE: 88   FOR A TEA PARTY: 264

Apricot & Almond Layer Cake

SERVES 8–10

150 g/5 oz unsalted
   butter, softened
125 g/4 oz caster sugar
5 medium eggs, separated
150 g/5 oz dark chocolate,
   melted and cooled

150 g/5 oz self-raising
   flour, sifted
50 g/2 oz ground almonds
75 g/3 oz icing sugar, sifted
300 g/11 oz apricot jam
1 tbsp amaretto liqueur

125 g/4 oz unsalted
   butter, melted
125 g/4 oz dark chocolate,
   melted

Preheat the oven to 180°C/350°F/Gas Mark 4, 10 minutes before baking. Lightly oil and line two 23 cm/9 inch round cake tins. Cream the butter and sugar together until light and fluffy, then beat in the egg yolks, one at a time, beating well after each addition. Stir in the cooled chocolate with 1 tablespoon cooled boiled water, then fold in the flour and ground almonds.

Whisk the egg whites until stiff, then gradually whisk in the icing sugar, beating well after each addition. Whisk until the egg whites are stiff and glossy, then fold the egg whites into the chocolate mixture in two batches.

Divide the mixture evenly between the tins and bake in the preheated oven for 30–40 minutes until firm. Leave for 5 minutes before turning out onto wire racks. Leave to cool completely.

Split the cakes in half. Gently heat the jam, pass through a sieve and stir in the amaretto liqueur. Place one cake layer onto a serving plate. Spread with a little of the jam, then sandwich with the next layer. Repeat with all the layers and use any remaining jam to brush over the entire cake. Leave until the jam sets.

Meanwhile, beat the butter and chocolate together until smooth, then cool at room temperature until thick enough to spread. Cover the top and sides of the cake with the chocolate icing and leave to set before slicing and serving.

Try this: FOR AN ALTERNATIVE: 48   FOR A TEA PARTY: 206

Mocha Truffle Cake

**CUTS INTO
8–10 SLICES**

3 medium eggs
125 g/4 oz caster sugar
40 g/1½ oz cornflour
40 g/1½ oz self-raising flour
2 tbsp cocoa powder
2 tbsp milk

2 tbsp coffee liqueur
100 g/3½ oz white chocolate,
    melted and cooled
200 g/7 oz dark chocolate,
    melted and cooled
600 ml/1 pint double cream

200 g/7 oz milk chocolate
100 g/3½ oz unsalted butter

Preheat the oven to 180˚C/350˚F/Gas Mark 4, 10 minutes before baking. Lightly oil and line a deep, 23 cm/9 inch, round cake tin. Beat the eggs and sugar in a bowl until thick and creamy. Sift together the cornflour, self-raising flour and cocoa powder and fold lightly into the egg mixture. Spoon into the tin and bake in the preheated oven for 30 minutes, or until firm. Turn out onto a wire rack and leave until cold. Split the cold cake horizontally into two layers. Mix together the milk and coffee liqueur and brush onto the cake layers.

Stir the cooled white chocolate into one bowl and the cooled dark chocolate into another one. Whip the cream until soft peaks form, then divide between the two bowls and stir. Place one layer of cake in a 23 cm/9 inch springform tin. Spread with half the white chocolate cream. Top with the dark chocolate cream, then the remaining white chocolate cream. Finally, place the remaining cake layer on top. Chill in the refrigerator for 4 hours, or overnight, until set.

When ready to serve, melt the milk chocolate and butter in a heatproof bowl set over a saucepan of simmering water and stir until smooth. Remove from the heat and leave until thick enough to spread, then use to cover the top and sides of the cake. Leave to set at room temperature, then chill in the refrigerator. Cut the cake into slices and serve.

Try this: FOR AN ALTERNATIVE: 82   FOR A TEA PARTY: 250

Peach & White Chocolate Gateau

SERVES 8–10

175 g/6 oz unsalted
   butter, softened
2 tsp grated orange zest
175 g/6 oz caster sugar
3 medium eggs
100 g/3½ oz white chocolate,
   melted and cooled

225 g/8 oz self-raising
   flour, sifted
300 ml/½ pint double cream
40 g/1½ oz icing sugar
125 g/4 oz hazelnuts, toasted
   and chopped

For the peach filling:
2 ripe peaches, peeled
   and chopped
2 tbsp peach or orange
   liqueur
300 ml/½ pint double cream
40 g/1½ oz icing sugar

Preheat the oven to 170°C/325°F/Gas Mark 3, 10 minutes before baking. Lightly oil and line a deep, 23 cm/9 inch, round cake tin. Cream the butter, orange zest and sugar together until light and fluffy. Add the eggs, one at a time, beating well after each addition, then beat in the cooled white chocolate.

Add the flour and 175 ml/6 fl oz water in two batches. Spoon into the prepared tin and bake in the preheated oven for 1½ hours, or until firm. Leave to stand for at least 5 minutes before turning out onto a wire rack to cool completely.

To make the filling, place the peaches in a bowl and pour over the liqueur. Leave to stand for 30 minutes. Whip the cream with the icing sugar until soft peaks form, then fold in the peach mixture.

Split the cold cake into three layers, place one layer on a serving plate and spread with half the peach filling. Top with a second sponge layer and spread with the remaining peach filling. Top with the remaining cake layer.

Whip the cream and icing sugar together until soft peaks form. Spread over the top and sides of the cake, piping some onto the top, if liked. Press the hazelnuts into the sides of the cake and, if liked, sprinkle a few on top. Chill in the refrigerator until required. Serve cut into slices. Store the cake in the refrigerator.

Try this: FOR AN ALTERNATIVE: 94 FOR A TEA PARTY: 200

Chocolate Buttermilk Cake

**CUTS INTO
8–10 SLICES**

175 g/6 oz butter
1 tsp vanilla extract
350 g/12 oz caster sugar
4 medium eggs, separated

100 g/3½ oz self-raising flour
40 g/1½ oz cocoa powder
175 ml/6 fl oz buttermilk
200 g/7 oz dark chocolate

100 g/3½ oz butter
300 ml/½ pint double cream

Preheat the oven to 180°C/350°F/Gas Mark 4, 10 minutes before baking. Lightly oil and line a deep, 23 cm/9 inch, round cake tin. Cream together the butter, vanilla extract and sugar until light and fluffy, then beat in the egg yolks, one at a time.

Sift together the flour and cocoa powder and fold into the egg mixture together with the buttermilk. Whisk the egg whites until soft peaks form and fold carefully into the chocolate mixture in two batches. Spoon the mixture into the prepared tin and bake in the preheated oven for 1 hour, or until firm. Cool slightly, then turn out onto a wire rack and leave until completely cold.

Place the chocolate and butter together in a heatproof bowl set over a saucepan of simmering water and heat until melted. Stir until smooth, then leave at room temperature until the chocolate is thick enough to spread.

Split the cake horizontally in half. Use some of the chocolate mixture to sandwich the two halves together. Spread and decorate the top of the cake with the remaining chocolate mixture. Finally, whip the cream until soft peaks form and use to spread around the sides of the cake. Chill in the refrigerator until required. Serve cut into slices. Store in the refrigerator.

Try this: FOR AN ALTERNATIVE: 96   FOR A TEA PARTY: 198

Dark Chocolate Layered Torte

**CUTS INTO
10–12 SLICES**

175 g/6 oz butter
1 tbsp instant coffee granules
150 g/5 oz dark chocolate
350 g/12 oz caster sugar
150 g/5 oz self-raising flour
125 g/4 oz plain flour

2 tbsp cocoa powder
2 medium eggs
1 tsp vanilla extract
215 g/7½ oz dark chocolate, melted
125 g/4 oz butter, melted

40 g/1½ oz icing sugar, sifted
2 tsp raspberry jam
2½ tbsp chocolate liqueur
100 g/3½ oz toasted flaked almonds

Preheat the oven to 150°C/300°F/Gas Mark 2, 10 minutes before baking. Lightly oil and line a 23 cm/9 inch square cake tin. Melt the butter in a saucepan, remove from the heat and stir in the coffee granules and 225 ml/8 fl oz hot water. Add the dark chocolate and sugar and stir until smooth, then pour into a bowl. In another bowl, sift together the flours and cocoa powder. Using an electric whisk, beat the sifted mixture into the chocolate mixture until smooth. Beat in the eggs and vanilla extract. Pour into the tin and bake in the preheated oven for 1¼ hours, or until firm. Leave for at least 5 minutes before turning out onto a wire rack to cool.

Mix together 200 g/7 oz of the melted dark chocolate with the butter and icing sugar and beat until smooth. Leave to cool, then beat again. Reserve 4–5 tablespoons of the chocolate filling. Cut the cooled cake in half to make two rectangles, then split each rectangle horizontally into three. Place one cake layer on a serving plate and spread thinly with the jam, then a thin layer of dark chocolate filling. Top with a second cake layer and sprinkle with a little liqueur, then spread thinly with filling. Repeat with the remaining cake layers, liqueur and filling.

Chill in the refrigerator for 2–3 hours until firm. Cover the cake with the reserved chocolate filling and press the flaked almonds into the sides of the cake. Place the remaining melted chocolate in a nonstick baking parchment piping bag. Snip a small hole in the tip and pipe thin lines 2 cm/¾ inch apart crossways over the cake. Drag a cocktail stick lengthways through the icing in alternating directions to create a feathered effect on the top. Serve.

Try this: FOR AN ALTERNATIVE: 112   FOR A TEA PARTY: 214

Chocolate Mousse Sponge

**CUTS INTO
8–10 SLICES**

3 medium eggs
75 g/3 oz caster sugar
1 tsp vanilla extract
50 g/2 oz self-raising
   flour, sifted
25 g/1 oz ground almonds
50 g/2 oz dark chocolate,
   grated

icing sugar, for dusting
freshly sliced strawberries,
   to decorate

For the mousse:
2 sheets gelatine
50 ml/2 fl oz double cream

100 g/3½ oz dark chocolate,
   chopped
1 tsp vanilla extract
4 medium egg whites
125 g/4 oz caster sugar

Preheat the oven to 180°C/350°F/Gas Mark 4, 10 minutes before baking. Lightly oil and line a 23 cm/9 inch round cake tin and lightly oil the sides of a 23 cm/9 inch springform tin. Whisk the eggs, sugar and vanilla extract together until thick and creamy. Fold in the flour, ground almonds and dark chocolate. Spoon the mixture into the prepared round cake tin and bake in the preheated oven for 25 minutes, or until firm. Turn out onto a wire rack to cool.

For the mousse, soak the gelatine in 50 ml/2 fl oz cold water for 5 minutes until softened. Meanwhile, heat the double cream in a small saucepan. When almost boiling, remove from the heat and stir in the chocolate and vanilla extract. Stir until the chocolate melts. Squeeze the excess water out of the gelatine and add to the chocolate mixture. Stir until dissolved, then pour into a large bowl.

Whisk the egg whites until stiff, then gradually add the caster sugar, whisking well after each addition. Fold the egg white mixture into the chocolate mixture in two batches. Split the cake into two layers. Place one layer in the bottom of the springform tin. Pour in the mousse mixture, then top with the second layer of cake. Chill in the refrigerator for 4 hours, or until the mousse has set. Loosen the sides and remove the cake from the tin. Dust with icing sugar and decorate the top with a few freshly sliced strawberries. Serve cut into slices.

Try this: FOR AN ALTERNATIVE: 50   FOR A TEA PARTY: 258

Chocolate Hazelnut Meringue Gateau

**CUTS INTO
8–10 SLICES**

5 medium egg whites
275 g/10 oz caster sugar
125 g/4 oz hazelnuts, toasted
and finely chopped
175 g/6 oz dark chocolate

100 g/3½ oz butter
3 medium eggs, separated,
plus 1 medium egg white
25 g/1 oz icing sugar
125 ml/4 fl oz double cream

hazelnuts, toasted and
chopped, to decorate

Preheat the oven to 150°C/300°F/Gas Mark 2, 5 minutes before baking. Cut three pieces of baking parchment into 30.5 cm x 12.5 cm/12 inch x 5 inch rectangles and then place onto two or three baking sheets. Whisk the egg whites until stiff, add half the sugar and whisk until stiff, smooth and glossy. Whisk in the remaining sugar, 1 tablespoon at a time, beating well after each addition. When all the sugar has been added, whisk for 1 minute. Stir in the nuts. Spoon the meringue inside the rectangles, spreading in a continuous backwards and forwards movement. Bake in the preheated oven for 1¼ hours, remove and leave until cold. Trim the meringues until they measure 25.5 cm x 10 cm/10 inches x 4 inches. Reserve the trimmings.

Melt the chocolate and the butter in a heatproof bowl set over a saucepan of gently simmering water and stir until smooth. Remove from the heat and beat in the egg yolks. Whisk the egg whites until stiff, then whisk in the icing sugar a little at a time. Fold the whites into the chocolate mixture and chill for 20–30 minutes until thick enough to spread. Whip the double cream until soft peaks form. Reserve. Place one of the meringue layers onto a serving plate. Spread with about half of the mousse mixture, then top with a second meringue layer. Spread the remaining mousse mixture over the top with the third meringue. Spread the cream over the top and sprinkle with the chopped hazelnuts. Chill in the refrigerator for at least 4 hours and up to 24 hours. Serve cut into slices.

Try this: FOR AN ALTERNATIVE: 102 FOR A TEA PARTY: 198

French Chocolate Pecan Torte

**CUTS INTO
16 SLICES**

200 g/7 oz dark chocolate, chopped
150 g/5 oz butter, diced
4 large eggs
100 g/3½ oz caster sugar
2 tsp vanilla extract

125 g/4 oz pecans, finely ground
2 tsp ground cinnamon
24 pecan halves, lightly toasted, to decorate

For the chocolate glaze:
125 g/4 oz dark chocolate, chopped
65 g/2½ oz butter, diced
2 tbsp clear honey
¼ tsp ground cinnamon

Preheat the oven to 180°C/350°F/Gas Mark 4, 10 minutes before baking. Lightly butter and line a 20.5 x 5 cm/8 x 2 inch springform tin with nonstick baking parchment. Wrap the tin in a large sheet of foil to prevent water seeping in.

Melt the chocolate and butter in a saucepan over a low heat and stir until smooth. Remove from the heat and cool. Using an electric whisk, beat the eggs, sugar and vanilla extract together until light and foamy. Gradually beat in the melted chocolate, ground nuts and cinnamon, then pour into the tin.

Set the foil-wrapped tin in a large roasting tin and pour in enough boiling water to come 2 cm/ ¾ inch up the sides of the tin. Bake in the preheated oven until the edge is set but the centre is still soft when the tin is gently shaken. Remove from the oven and place on a wire rack to cool.

For the glaze, melt all the ingredients together over a low heat until melted and smooth, then remove from the heat. Dip each pecan halfway into the glaze and set on a sheet of nonstick baking parchment until set. Allow the remaining glaze to thicken slightly.

Remove the cake from the tin and invert. Pour the glaze over the cake, smoothing the top and spreading the glaze around the sides. Arrange the glazed pecans around the edge of the torte. Allow to set and then serve.

Try this: FOR AN ALTERNATIVE: 74 FOR A TEA PARTY: 228

Whole Orange & Chocolate Cake with Marmalade Cream

SERVES 6–8

1 small orange, scrubbed
2 medium eggs, separated,
   plus 1 whole egg
150 g/5 oz caster sugar
125 g/4 oz ground almonds

75 g/3 oz dark chocolate,
   melted
100 ml/3½ fl oz double cream
200 g/7 oz full-fat soft cheese
25 g/1 oz icing sugar

2 tbsp orange marmalade
orange zest, to decorate

Preheat the oven to 180°C/350°F/Gas Mark 4, 10 minutes before baking. Lightly oil and line the base of a 900 g/2 lb loaf tin. Place the orange in a small saucepan, cover with cold water and bring to the boil. Simmer for 1 hour until completely soft. Drain and leave to cool. Place 2 egg yolks, 1 whole egg and the sugar in a heatproof bowl set over a saucepan of simmering water and whisk until doubled in bulk. Remove from the heat and continue to whisk for 5 minutes until cooled.

Cut the whole orange in half and discard the seeds, then place into a food processor or blender and blend to a purée. Carefully fold the purée into the egg yolk mixture with the ground almonds and melted chocolate. Whisk the egg whites until stiff peaks form. Fold a large spoonful of the egg whites into the chocolate mixture, then gently fold the remaining egg whites into the mixture.

Pour into the tin and bake in the preheated oven for 50 minutes, or until firm and a skewer inserted into the centre comes out clean. Cool in the tin before turning out and carefully discarding the lining paper. Meanwhile, whip the double cream until just thickened. In another bowl, blend the soft cheese with the icing sugar and marmalade until smooth, then fold in the double cream. Chill the marmalade cream in the refrigerator until required. Decorate with orange zest and serve the cake cut into slices with the marmalade cream.

Try this: FOR AN ALTERNATIVE: 70 FOR A TEA PARTY: 194

White Chocolate & Raspberry Mousse Gateau

CUTS INTO 8 SLICES

4 medium eggs
125 g/4 oz caster sugar
75 g/3 oz plain flour, sifted
25 g/1 oz cornflour, sifted
3 gelatine leaves
450 g/1 lb raspberries,
   thawed if frozen

400 g/14 oz white chocolate
200 g/7 oz plain
   fromage frais
2 medium egg whites
25 g/1 oz caster sugar
4 tbsp raspberry or orange
   liqueur

200 ml/7 fl oz double cream
fresh raspberries, halved,
   to decorate

Preheat the oven to 190°C/375°F/Gas Mark 5, 10 minutes before baking. Oil and line two 23 cm/9 inch cake tins. Whisk the eggs and sugar together until thick and creamy and the whisk leaves a trail in the mixture. Fold in the flour and cornflour, then divide between the tins. Bake in the preheated oven for 12–15 minutes until risen and firm. Cool in the tins, then turn out onto wire racks.

Place the gelatine with 4 tablespoons cold water in a dish and leave to soften for 5 minutes. Purée half the raspberries, press through a sieve, then heat until nearly boiling. Squeeze out excess water from the gelatine, add to the purée and stir until dissolved. Reserve. Melt 175 g/6 oz of the chocolate in a bowl set over a saucepan of simmering water. Leave to cool, then stir in the fromage frais and purée. Whisk the egg whites until stiff and whisk in the sugar. Fold into the raspberry mixture with the raspberries. Line the sides of a 23 cm/9 inch springform tin with baking parchment. Place one layer of cake in the base and sprinkle with half the liqueur. Pour in the raspberry mixture and top with the second cake. Brush with the remaining liqueur. Press down and chill for 4 hours. Unmould onto a plate. Cut a strip of double thickness baking parchment to fit around and 1 cm/½ inch higher than the cake. Melt the remaining chocolate and spread thickly onto the parchment. Leave until just setting. Wrap around the cake and freeze for 15 minutes. Peel away the parchment. Whip the cream until thick and spread over the top. Decorate with raspberries.

Try this: FOR AN ALTERNATIVE: 40   FOR A TEA PARTY: 196

CUTS INTO
8–10 SLICES

Chocolate Orange Fudge Cake

65 g/2½ oz cocoa powder
grated zest of 1 orange
350 g/12 oz self-raising flour
2 tsp baking powder
1 tsp bicarbonate of soda
½ tsp salt

225 g/8 oz soft light
  brown sugar
175 g/6 oz butter, softened
3 medium eggs
1 tsp vanilla extract
275 ml/9 fl oz sour cream

6 tbsp butter
6 tbsp milk
thinly pared rind of 1 orange
6 tbsp cocoa powder
250 g/9 oz icing sugar, sifted

Preheat the oven to 180°C/350°F/Gas Mark 4, 10 minutes before baking. Lightly oil and line two 23 cm/9 inch round cake tins with nonstick baking parchment. Blend the cocoa powder and 50 ml/2 fl oz boiling water until smooth. Stir in the orange zest and reserve. Sift together the flour, baking powder, bicarbonate of soda and salt, then reserve. Cream together the sugar and softened butter and beat in the eggs, one at a time, then the cocoa mixture and vanilla extract. Finally, stir in the flour mixture and the sour cream in alternate spoonfuls.

Divide the mixture between the prepared tins and bake in the preheated oven for 35 minutes, or until the edges of the cake pull away from the tin and the tops spring back when lightly pressed. Cool in the tins for 10 minutes, then turn out onto wire racks to cool.

Gently heat together the butter and milk with the pared orange rind. Simmer for 10 minutes, stirring occasionally. Remove from the heat and discard the orange rind.

Pour the warm orange and milk mixture into a large bowl and stir in the cocoa powder. Gradually beat in the sifted icing sugar and beat until the icing is smooth and spreadable. Place one cake onto a large serving plate. Top with about one quarter of the icing, place the second cake on top, then cover the cake completely with the remaining icing. Serve.

Try this: FOR AN ALTERNATIVE: 92   FOR A TEA PARTY: 264

Italian Polenta Cake
with Mascarpone Cream

**CUTS INTO
6–8 SLICES**

1 tsp butter and flour for
   the tin
100 g/3½ oz plain flour
40 g/1½ oz polenta or
   yellow cornmeal
1 tsp baking powder
¼ tsp salt
grated zest of 1 lemon
2 large eggs

150 g/5 oz caster sugar
5 tbsp milk
½ tsp almond extract
2 tbsp raisins or sultanas
75 g/3 oz unsalted butter,
   softened
2 medium dessert pears,
   peeled, cored and
   thinly sliced

2 tbsp apricot jam
175 g/6 oz mascarpone cheese
1–2 tsp sugar
50 ml/2 fl oz double cream
2 tbsp amaretto liqueur or
   rum
2–3 tbsp toasted flaked
   almonds
icing sugar, for dusting

Preheat the oven to 190°C/375°F/Gas Mark 5, 10 minutes before baking. Butter a 23 cm/
9 inch springform tin. Dust lightly with flour. Stir the flour, polenta or cornmeal, baking powder,
salt and lemon zest together. Beat the eggs and half the sugar together until light and fluffy.
Slowly beat in the milk and almond extract.

Stir in the raisins or sultanas, then beat in the flour mixture and 50 g/2 oz of the butter. Spoon into
the tin and smooth the top evenly. Arrange the pear slices on top in overlapping concentric circles.

Melt the remaining butter and brush over the pear slices. Sprinkle with the rest of the sugar.
Bake in the preheated oven for about 40 minutes until puffed and golden and the edges of
the pears are lightly caramelised. Transfer to a wire rack. Reserve to cool in the tin for
15 minutes. Remove the cake from the tin. Heat the apricot jam with 1 tablespoon water
and brush over the top of the cake to glaze.

Beat the mascarpone cheese with the sugar to taste, the cream and amaretto or rum until
smooth and forming a soft dropping consistency. When cool, sprinkle the almonds over the
polenta cake and dust generously with the icing sugar. Serve the cake with the liqueur-
flavoured mascarpone cream on the side.

Try this: FOR AN ALTERNATIVE: 52 FOR A TEA PARTY: 220

Coffee & Walnut Gateau with Brandied Prunes

**CUTS INTO
10–12 SLICES**

For the prunes:
225 g/8 oz ready-to-eat pitted
   dried prunes
150 ml/¼ pint cold tea
3 tbsp brandy

For the cake:
450 g/1 lb walnut pieces

50 g/2 oz self-raising flour
½ tsp baking powder
1 tsp instant coffee powder
   (not granules)
5 large eggs, separated
¼ tsp cream of tartar
150 g/5 oz caster sugar
2 tbsp sunflower oil

8 walnut halves, to decorate

For the filling:
600 ml/1 pint double cream
4 tbsp icing sugar, sifted
2 tbsp coffee-flavoured
   liqueur

Preheat the oven to 180°C/350°F/Gas Mark 4, 10 minutes before baking. Soak the prunes with the tea and brandy for 3–4 hours, or overnight. Oil and line the bases of two 23 cm/ 9 inch tins. Chop the walnuts in a food processor and reserve one quarter. Add the flour, baking powder and coffee to the walnuts still in the processor and blend until finely ground.

Whisk the egg whites with the cream of tartar until soft peaks form. Sprinkle in one third of the sugar, 2 tablespoons at a time, until stiff peaks form. In another bowl, beat the egg yolks, oil and the remaining sugar until thick. Alternately fold in the nut mixture and egg whites until just blended. Divide the mixture evenly between the tins, smoothing the tops. Bake in the oven for 30–35 minutes until the tops of the cakes spring back when lightly pressed with a clean finger. Remove from the oven and cool. Remove from the tins and discard the lining paper.

Drain the prunes, reserving the liquid. Dry on kitchen paper, then chop and reserve. Whisk the cream with the icing sugar and liqueur until soft peaks form. Spoon one eighth of the cream into a pastry bag fitted with a star nozzle. Cut the cake layers in half horizontally. Sprinkle each cut side with 1 tablespoon of the reserved prune-soaking liquid. Sandwich the cakes together with half of the cream and all of the prunes. Spread the remaining cream around the sides and press in the reserved chopped walnuts. Pipe rosettes around the edge, decorate with walnut halves and serve.

Try this: FOR AN ALTERNATIVE: 78   FOR A TEA PARTY: 226

Raspberry & Hazelnut Meringue Cake

CUTS INTO 8 SLICES

For the meringue:
4 large egg whites
¼ tsp cream of tartar
225 g/8 oz caster sugar
75 g/3 oz hazelnuts, skinned,
    toasted and finely ground

For the filling:
300 ml/½ pint double cream
1 tbsp icing sugar
1–2 tbsp raspberry-flavoured
    liqueur (optional)
350 g/12 oz fresh raspberries

Preheat the oven to 140°C/275°F/Gas Mark 1, 10 minutes before baking. Line two baking sheets with nonstick baking parchment and draw a 20.5 cm/8 inch circle on each. Whisk the egg whites and cream of tartar together until soft peaks form, then gradually beat in the sugar, 2 tablespoons at a time.

Beat well after each addition until the whites are stiff and glossy. Using a metal spoon or rubber spatula, gently fold in the ground hazelnuts.

Divide the mixture evenly between the two circles and spread neatly. Swirl one of the circles to make a decorative top layer. Bake in the preheated oven for about $1^1/_2$ hours until crisp and dry. Turn off the oven and allow the meringues to cool for 1 hour. Transfer to a wire rack to cool completely. Carefully peel off the papers.

For the filling, whip the cream, icing sugar and liqueur, if using, together until soft peaks form. Place the flat round on a serving plate. Spread over most of the cream, reserving some for decorating, and arrange the raspberries in concentric circles over the cream.

Place the swirly meringue on top of the cream and raspberries, pressing down gently. Pipe the remaining cream onto the meringue and decorate with a few raspberries, then serve.

Try this: FOR AN ALTERNATIVE: 88   FOR A TEA PARTY: 196

Chocolate Mousse Cake

**CUTS INTO
8–10 SLICES**

For the cake:
450 g/1 lb dark chocolate,
   chopped
125 g/4 oz butter, softened
3 tbsp brandy
9 large eggs, separated

150 g/5 oz caster sugar

For the chocolate glaze:
225 ml/8 fl oz double cream
225 g/8 oz dark chocolate,
   chopped

2 tbsp brandy
white chocolate curls,
   to decorate
1 tbsp single cream, to serve

Preheat the oven to 180°C/350°F/Gas Mark 4, 10 minutes before baking. Lightly oil and line the bases of two 20.5 cm/8 inch springform tins with baking parchment. Melt the chocolate and butter together in a bowl set over a saucepan of simmering water. Stir until smooth. Remove from the heat and stir in the brandy.

Whisk the egg yolks and all but 2 tablespoons of the sugar until thick and creamy. Slowly beat in the chocolate mixture until smooth and well blended. Whisk the egg whites until soft peaks form, then sprinkle over the remaining sugar and whisk until stiff but not dry. Fold a large spoonful of the whites into the chocolate. Gently fold in the rest. Divide about two thirds of the mixture evenly between the tins, tapping to distribute it evenly. Bake in the preheated oven for about 20 minutes until the cakes are well risen and set. Cool for at least 1 hour. Loosen the edges of the cake layers with a knife. Using the fingertips, lightly press the crusty edges down. Pour the rest of the mousse over one layer, spreading until even. Carefully unclip the side, remove the other cake from the tin and gently invert onto the mousse, bottom-side up. Discard the paper and chill for 4–6 hours until set.

To make the glaze, melt the cream and chocolate with the brandy in a heavy saucepan and stir until smooth. Cool until thickened. Unclip the side of the second tin and place the cake on a wire rack. Cover the cake with half the glaze. Allow to set, then decorate with chocolate curls. Serve with heated glaze and dotted with cream.

Try this: FOR AN ALTERNATIVE: 86 FOR A TEA PARTY: 190

Chocolate & Almond Daquoise with Summer Berries

CUTS INTO 8 SLICES

For the almond meringues:
6 large egg whites
¼ tsp cream of tartar
275 g/10 oz caster sugar
½ tsp almond extract
50 g/2 oz blanched or flaked almonds, lightly toasted and finely ground

For the chocolate buttercream:
75 g/3 oz butter, softened
450 g/1 lb icing sugar, sifted
50 g/2 oz cocoa powder, sifted
3–4 tbsp milk or single cream

550 g/1 lb 3 oz mixed summer berries, such as raspberries, strawberries and blackberries

To decorate:
toasted flaked almonds
icing sugar

Preheat the oven to 140°C/275°F/Gas Mark 1, 10 minutes before baking. Line three baking sheets with nonstick baking parchment and draw a 20.5 cm/8 inch round on each one.

Whisk the egg whites and cream of tartar until soft peaks form. Gradually beat in the sugar, 2 tablespoons at a time, beating well after each addition, until the whites are stiff and glossy.

Beat in the almond extract, then, using a metal spoon or rubber spatula, gently fold in the ground almonds. Divide the mixture evenly between the three circles of baking paper, spreading neatly into the rounds and smoothing the tops evenly. Bake in the preheated oven for about 1¼ hours until crisp, rotating the baking sheets halfway through cooking. Turn off the oven, allow to cool for about 1 hour, then remove and cool completely before discarding the lining paper.

Beat the butter, icing sugar and cocoa powder together until smooth and creamy, adding the milk or cream to form a soft consistency. Reserve about a quarter of the berries to decorate. Spread one meringue with a third of the buttercream and top with a third of the remaining berries. Repeat with the other meringue rounds, buttercream and berries. Scatter with the toasted flaked almonds and the reserved berries and sprinkle with icing sugar, then serve.

Try this: FOR AN ALTERNATIVE: 76   FOR A TEA PARTY: 212

Ricotta Cheesecake with Strawberry Coulis

SERVES 6–8

125 g/4 oz digestive biscuits
100 g/3½ oz candied peel, chopped
65 g/2½ oz butter, melted
150 ml/¼ pint crème fraîche

575 g/1¼ lb ricotta cheese
100 g/3½ oz caster sugar
1 vanilla pod, seeds only
2 large eggs
225 g/8 oz strawberries

25–50 g/1–2 oz caster sugar, or to taste
zest and juice of 1 orange

Preheat the oven to 170°C/325°F/Gas Mark 3, 10 minutes before baking. Line a 20.5 cm/8 inch springform tin with baking parchment. Place the biscuits into a food processor together with the peel. Blend until the biscuits are crushed and the peel is chopped. Add 50 g/2 oz of the melted butter and process until mixed. Tip into the tin and spread evenly over the bottom. Press firmly into place and reserve.

Blend together the crème fraîche, ricotta cheese, sugar, vanilla seeds and eggs in a food processor. With the motor running, add the remaining melted butter and blend for a few seconds. Pour the mixture onto the base. Transfer to the preheated oven and cook for about 1 hour until set and risen round the edges, but slightly wobbly in the centre. Switch off the oven and allow to cool there. Chill in the refrigerator for at least 8 hours, or preferably overnight.

Wash and drain the strawberries. Hull the fruit and remove any soft spots. Put into the food processor along with 25 g/1 oz of the sugar and the orange juice and zest. Blend until smooth. Add any remaining sugar to taste. Pass through a sieve to remove seeds and chill in the refrigerator until needed.

Cut the cheesecake into wedges, spoon over some of the strawberry coulis and serve.

Try this: FOR AN ALTERNATIVE: 36 FOR A TEA PARTY: 204

Orange Fruit Cake

SERVES 6

For the orange cake:
225 g/8 oz self-raising flour
2 tsp baking powder
225 g/8 oz caster sugar
225 g/8 oz butter, softened
4 large eggs
grated zest of 1 orange
2 tbsp orange juice
2–3 tbsp Cointreau

125 g/4 oz chopped nuts
Cape gooseberries,
　blueberries, raspberries
　and mint sprigs,
　to decorate
icing sugar, for dusting
　(optional)

For the filling:
450 ml/¾ pint double cream
50 ml/2 fl oz Greek yogurt
½ tsp vanilla extract
2–3 tbsp Cointreau
1 tbsp icing sugar
450 g/1 lb orange fruits, such
　as mango, peach, papaya,
　nectarine, yellow plums

Preheat the oven to 180°C/350°F/Gas Mark 4, 10 minutes before baking. Lightly oil and line the base of a 25.5 cm/10 inch deep cake tin or springform tin with nonstick baking parchment.

Sift the flour and baking powder into a large bowl and stir in the sugar. Make a well in the centre and add the butter, eggs, grated zest and orange juice. Beat until blended and a smooth batter is formed. Turn into the tin and smooth the top.

Bake in the oven for 35–45 minutes until golden and the sides begin to shrink from the edge of the tin. Remove, cool before removing from the tin and discard the lining paper. Using a serrated knife, slice off the top third of cake, cutting horizontally. Sprinkle the cut sides with the Cointreau.

To make the filling, whip the cream and yogurt with the vanilla extract, Cointreau and icing sugar until soft peaks form. Chop the orange fruit and fold into the cream. Spread some of this mixture onto the bottom cake layer. Transfer to a serving plate.

Cover with the top layer of sponge and spread the remaining cream mixture over the top and sides. Press the chopped nuts into the sides of the cake and decorate the top with the Cape gooseberries, blueberries, raspberries and mint. If liked, dust the top with icing sugar, then serve.

Try this: FOR AN ALTERNATIVE: 40 FOR A TEA PARTY: 232

Black & White Torte

SERVES 8–10

4 medium eggs	150 g/5 oz dark chocolate,
150 g/5 oz caster sugar	chopped
50 g/2 oz cornflour	6 tbsp Grand Marnier, or
50 g/2 oz plain flour	other orange liqueur
50 g/2 oz self-raising flour	300 g/11 oz white chocolate,
900 ml/1½ pints double	chopped
cream	cocoa powder, for dusting

Preheat the oven to 180°C/350°F/Gas Mark 4, 10 minutes before baking. Lightly oil and line a 23 cm/9 inch round cake tin. Beat the eggs and sugar in a large bowl until thick and creamy. Sift together the cornflour, plain flour and self-raising flour three times, then lightly fold into the egg mixture. Spoon the mixture into the tin and bake in the preheated oven for 35–40 minutes until firm. Turn the cake out onto a wire rack and leave to cool.

Place 300 ml/½ pint of the double cream in a saucepan and bring to the boil. Remove from the heat and add the dark chocolate and 1 tablespoon of the liqueur. Stir until smooth. Repeat using the remaining cream, white chocolate and 2 tablespoons of the liqueur. Refrigerate for 2 hours, then whisk each mixture until thick and creamy.

Place the dark chocolate mixture in a piping bag fitted with a plain nozzle and place half the white chocolate mixture in a separate piping bag fitted with a plain nozzle. Reserve the remaining white chocolate mixture.

Split the cold cake horizontally into two layers. Brush or drizzle the remaining 3 tablespoons of the liqueur over the cakes. Put one layer onto a plate. Pipe alternating rings of white and dark chocolate mixture to cover the first layer of cake. Use the reserved white chocolate mixture to cover the top and sides of the cake. Dust with cocoa powder, cut into slices and serve.

Try this: FOR AN ALTERNATIVE: 54 FOR A TEA PARTY: 236

Special Occasions

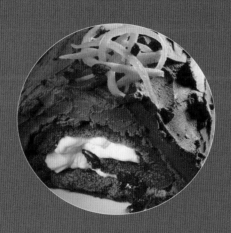

Christmas Cake

SERVES 12–14

900 g/2 lb mixed dried fruit
75 g/3 oz glacé cherries,
　rinsed and halved
3 tbsp brandy or orange juice
finely grated zest and juice
　of 1 lemon
225 g/8 oz soft dark
　muscovado sugar

225 g/8 oz butter
4 medium eggs, beaten
225 g/8 oz plain flour
1 tbsp black treacle
1 tbsp mixed spice

To decorate:
2–4 tbsp brandy (optional)

4 tbsp sieved apricot jam
700 g/1½ lb almond paste
　(*see* page 26)
icing sugar, for dusting
1 kg/2 lb 3 oz ready-to-roll
　sugarpaste
bought decorations
　and ribbon

Place the dried fruit and cherries in a bowl and sprinkle over the brandy or orange juice and the lemon zest and juice. Stir and let soak for 2–4 hours. Preheat the oven to 150˚C/300˚F/ Gas Mark 2. Grease and double-line the base and sides of a 20.5 cm/8 inch, deep, round cake tin. Beat the sugar and butter together until soft and fluffy. Beat the eggs in gradually, adding 1 teaspoon of the flour with each addition. Stir in the treacle, then sift in the rest of the flour and the spice. Add the soaked fruit and stir until the mixture is smooth. Spoon into the tin and smooth the top level. Bake for 1 hour, then reduce the temperature to 140˚C/275˚F/ Gas Mark 1 and bake for a further 2–2½ hours until a skewer inserted into the centre comes out clean. Leave the cake to cool in the tin. When completely cold, remove and wrap in greaseproof paper and then in foil and store in a cool place for 1–3 months.

To decorate, brush the cake all over with brandy, if using. Heat the jam and brush over the top and sides. Roll out one third of the almond paste and cut into a disc the size of the top of the cake, using the empty tin as a guide. Place the disc on top. Roll the remaining paste into a strip long enough to cover the sides of the cake and press on. Leave the almond paste to dry out in a cool place for 2 days. On a surface dusted with icing sugar, roll out the sugarpaste to a circle large enough to cover the top and sides of the cake. Brush 1 tablespoon brandy or cold boiled water over the almond paste and place the sugarpaste on top. Smooth down and trim. Make a border from tiny balls of sugarpaste and decorate.

　　　Try this: FOR AN ALTERNATIVE: 166　FOR A TEA PARTY: 260

Golden Wedding Celebration Cupcakes

MAKES 24

125 g/4 oz self-raising flour
125 g/4 oz caster sugar
125 g/4 oz soft margarine
2 medium eggs, beaten
1 tsp lemon juice

To decorate:
125 g/4 oz buttercream
   (*see* page 24)
icing sugar, for dusting

700 g/1½ lb ready-to-roll
   sugarpaste
yellow paste food colouring
thin gold ribbon, curled

Preheat the oven to 180°C/350°F/Gas Mark 4, 10 minutes before baking. Line two 12-hole bun trays with small gold foil cases.

Sift the flour into a bowl and stir together with the caster sugar. Add the margarine and eggs and beat together with the lemon juice for about 2 minutes until smooth.

Spoon into the cases and bake for 15–20 minutes until golden and firm to the touch. Turn out on a wire rack. When cool, trim the tops flat if they have peaked slightly.

To decorate, lightly coat the top of each cupcake with a little buttercream. Dust a clean, flat surface with icing sugar. Roll out two thirds of the sugarpaste and stamp out circles 6 cm/2½ inches wide and place these on the buttercream to cover the top of each cupcake.

Colour one eighth of the sugarpaste a deep yellow and mould this into thin sausage shapes. Leave these to dry for about 2 hours until firm. Roll out the remaining white sugarpaste and mark out small squares 4 x 4 cm/¾ x ¾ inch. Wrap a square round a yellow centre to form a lily and press the ends together. Make up all the lilies and place on the cupcakes. Cut short, thin strips of gold paper ribbon and pull along the blade of a pair of scissors to curl, and place on the cakes. Keep for 3 days in an airtight container in a cool place. Remove the ribbons before eating.

Try this: FOR AN ALTERNATIVE: 144   FOR A TEA PARTY: 234

Valentine Heart Cupcakes

MAKES 12

150 g/5 oz butter, softened
150 g/5 oz caster sugar
3 medium eggs, beaten
1 tsp vanilla extract
2 tbsp milk
150 g/5 oz self-raising flour
½ tsp baking powder

To decorate:
225 g/8 oz ready-to-roll
   sugarpaste
pink and red paste food
   colouring
icing sugar, for dusting
1 batch cream cheese
   frosting (*see* page 24)

Preheat the oven to 180°C/350°F/Gas Mark 4, 10 minutes before baking and line a 12-hole muffin tray with deep paper cases.

Place the butter, sugar, eggs, vanilla extract and milk in a bowl, then sift in the flour and baking powder. Beat together for about 2 minutes with an electric hand mixer until pale and fluffy. Spoon into the paper cases and bake for 20–25 minutes until firm and golden. Cool on a wire rack.

To decorate, colour one third of the sugarpaste pink and one third red, leaving the rest white. Wrap a chopping board in clingfilm. Dust a clean, flat surface with icing sugar. Roll out the sugarpaste thinly and, using a cutter, cut out pink, red and white heart shapes, then leave to dry flat and harden for 2 hours (on the clingfilm-covered chopping board).

Colour the cream cheese frosting pale pink and place in a piping bag fitted with a star nozzle. Pipe a swirl on top of each cupcake and decorate with the hearts. Keep in a cool place for up to 2 days.

Try this: FOR AN ALTERNATIVE: 140   FOR A TEA PARTY: 238

Father's Day Cupcakes

MAKES 14

125 g/4 oz self-raising flour
125 g/4 oz caster sugar
125 g/4 oz soft margarine
2 medium eggs, beaten
1 tsp vanilla extract

To decorate:
1 batch buttercream
 (*see* page 24)
blue, yellow and orange
 paste food colouring

icing sugar, for dusting
225 g/8 oz ready-to-roll
 sugarpaste
50 g/2 oz royal icing sugar
edible silver balls

Preheat the oven to 180°C/350°F/Gas Mark 4, 10 minutes before baking. Line two 12-hole bun trays with 14 paper fairy-cake cases or silicone moulds.

Sift the flour into a bowl and stir together with the caster sugar. Add the margarine, eggs and vanilla extract and beat together for about 2 minutes until smooth.

Spoon into the cases and bake for 15–20 minutes until golden and firm to the touch. Turn out on a wire rack. When cool, trim the tops flat if they have peaked slightly.

To decorate, colour half the buttercream yellow and the other half orange and swirl over the top of each cupcake. Dust a clean, flat surface with icing sugar. Colour the sugarpaste light blue and roll out thinly. Stamp out large stars 4 cm/1½ inches wide and place these on the buttercream.

Make up the royal icing mix and place in a paper piping bag with the end snipped away and pipe 'Dad' or names on the stars. Decorate with the edible silver balls. Keep for 3 days in an airtight container.

Try this: FOR AN ALTERNATIVE: 158   FOR A TEA PARTY: 230

Christmas Cranberry Chocolate Roulade

CUTS INTO 12–14 SLICES

Chocolate ganache frosting:
300 ml/½ pint double cream
350 g/12 oz dark chocolate, chopped
2 tbsp brandy (optional)

For the roulade:
5 large eggs, separated

3 tbsp cocoa powder, sifted, plus extra for dusting
125 g/4 oz icing sugar, sifted, plus extra for dusting
¼ tsp cream of tartar

For the filling:
175 g/6 oz cranberry sauce

1–2 tbsp brandy (optional)
450 ml/¾ pint double cream, whipped to soft peaks

To decorate:
caramelised orange strips
dried cranberries

Preheat the oven to 200°C/400°F/Gas Mark 6, 10 minutes before baking. Bring the cream to the boil over a medium heat. Remove from the heat and add all of the chocolate, stirring until melted. Stir in the brandy, if using, and strain into a medium bowl. Cool. Refrigerate for 6–8 hours.

Lightly oil and line a 39 x 26 cm/151/2 x 10½ inch Swiss roll tin with nonstick baking parchment. Using an electric whisk, beat the egg yolks until thick and creamy. Slowly beat in the cocoa powder and half the icing sugar and reserve. Whisk the egg whites and cream of tartar into soft peaks. Gradually whisk in the remaining sugar until the mixture is stiff and glossy. Gently fold the yolk mixture into the egg whites. Spread evenly into the tin. Bake in the oven for 15 minutes. Remove and invert onto a sheet of greaseproof paper dusted with cocoa powder. Cut off the crisp edges of the cake, then roll up. Leave on a wire rack until cold.

For the filling, heat the cranberry sauce with the brandy, if using, until warm and spreadable. Unroll the cooled cake and spread with the cranberry sauce. Allow to cool and set. Carefully spoon the whipped cream over the surface and spread to within 2.5 cm/1 inch of the edges. Re-roll the cake. Transfer to a cake plate or tray. Allow the chocolate ganache to soften at room temperature, then beat until soft and of a spreadable consistency. Spread over the roulade and, using a fork, mark the roulade with ridges to resemble tree bark. Dust with icing sugar. Decorate with the caramelised orange strips and dried cranberries and serve.

Try this: FOR AN ALTERNATIVE: 176   FOR A TEA PARTY: 252

Christening Day Daisy Cupcakes

MAKES 12

150 g/5 oz butter, softened
150 g/5 oz caster sugar
150 g/5 oz self-raising flour
3 medium eggs, beaten
1 tsp lemon juice
2 tbsp milk

To decorate:
icing sugar, for dusting
125 g/4 oz sugarpaste
yellow gel icing tube
1 batch cream cheese
   frosting (*see* page 24)
yellow paste food colouring

Preheat the oven to 180°C/350°F/Gas Mark 4, 10 minutes before baking. Line a 12-hole muffin tray with deep paper cases.

Place the butter and sugar in a bowl, then sift in the flour. Add the beaten eggs to the bowl with the lemon juice and milk and beat until smooth. Spoon into the cases, filling them three-quarters full.

Bake for about 18 minutes until firm to the touch in the centre. Turn out to cool on a wire rack.

To decorate, dust a clean, flat surface with icing sugar. Roll out the sugarpaste thinly and stamp out daisy shapes. Leave these to dry out for 30 minutes until firm enough to handle. Pipe a small, yellow gel dot into the centre of each one. Colour the frosting pale yellow, then spread onto the cakes using a palette knife. Press the daisies onto the frosting. Keep in an airtight container in a cool place for 3 days.

Try this: FOR AN ALTERNATIVE: 150   FOR A TEA PARTY: 224

Pink Baby Bow Cupcakes

MAKES 12

125 g/4 oz self-raising flour
125 g/4 oz caster sugar
125 g/4 oz soft margarine
2 medium eggs, beaten
1 tsp vanilla extract
pink paste food colouring

To decorate:
1 batch buttercream
  (*see* page 24)
 pink paste food colouring
icing sugar, for dusting
225 g/8 oz ready-to-roll
  sugarpaste

Preheat the oven to 180°C/350°F/Gas Mark 4, 10 minutes before baking. Line a 12-hole muffin tray with deep paper cases or silicone moulds.

Sift the flour into a bowl and stir together with the caster sugar. Add the margarine, eggs and vanilla extract and beat together with a little pink paste food colouring to give a delicate pink. Beat for about 2 minutes until smooth. Spoon into the cases and bake for 20 minutes, or until golden and firm to the touch. Turn out on a wire rack. When cool, trim the tops flat if they have peaked slightly.

To decorate, colour the buttercream pale pink, then colour the sugarpaste pink to match the buttercream. Dust a clean, flat surface with icing sugar. Roll out the sugarpaste thinly and cut out long, narrow strips 1½ cm/½ inch wide. Roll small squares of nonstick baking parchment into narrow tubes and fold the pink icing over these to form loops. Make 24 loops, two for each cupcake, and leave to dry out and firm up for 2 hours. Cut strips to form the ribbon ends of each bow and keep aside on nonstick baking parchment.

To finish off the cupcakes, spread the top of each one with pink buttercream, carefully remove the loops from the paper and position the bows on the icing. Place the ribbon pieces onto the cupcakes to finish. Keep for 3 days in a cool place in an airtight container.

Try this: FOR AN ALTERNATIVE: 158 FOR A TEA PARTY: 222

Sparkly Christmas Cupcakes

MAKES 14–18

125 g/4 oz butter, softened
125 g/4 oz soft dark
    muscovado sugar
2 medium eggs, beaten
225 g/8 oz self-raising flour
1 tsp ground mixed spice
finely grated zest and 1 tbsp
    juice from 1 orange

1 tbsp black treacle
350 g/12 oz mixed dried fruit

To decorate:
3 tbsp sieved apricot glaze
    (*see* page 26)
225 g/8 oz almond paste
    (*see* page 26)

1 batch royal icing
    (*see* page 25)
edible silver ball decorations

Preheat the oven to 180°C/350°F/Gas Mark 4, 10 minutes before baking. Line a 12-hole bun tray with 14–18 foil fairy cake cases, depending on the size of the holes.

Beat the butter and sugar together until light and fluffy, then beat in the eggs a little at a time, adding 1 teaspoon flour with each addition. Sift in the remaining flour, and the spice, add the orange zest and juice, treacle and dried fruit to the bowl and fold together until the mixture is blended.

Spoon into the cases and bake for about 30 minutes until firm in the centre and a skewer inserted comes out clean. Leave to cool in the tins for 15 minutes, then turn out to cool on a wire rack. Store undecorated in an airtight container for up to 3 weeks, or freeze until needed.

To decorate, trim the top of each fairy cake level if they have peaked, then brush with apricot glaze. Roll out the almond paste and cut out eight circles. Place a disc on top of each fairy cake and press level. Leave to dry for 24 hours if possible.

Swirl the royal icing over the fairy cakes, flicking into peaks with a small palette knife. Decorate with silver balls while the icing is still wet. Leave to dry out for 1 hour.
Keep for 4 days in an airtight container.

Try this: FOR AN ALTERNATIVE: 178   FOR A TEA PARTY: 252

Celebration Fruit Cake

CUTS INTO 12 SLICES

125 g/4 oz butter or
    margarine
125 g/4 oz soft dark
    brown sugar
380 g can crushed pineapple
150 g/5 oz raisins
150 g/5 oz sultanas
125 g/4 oz crystallised
    ginger, chopped

125 g/4 oz glacé
    cherries, chopped
125 g/4 oz mixed cut peel
225 g/8 oz self-raising flour
1 tsp bicarbonate of soda
2 tsp mixed spice
1 tsp ground cinnamon
½ tsp salt
2 large eggs, beaten

For the topping:
100 g/3½ oz pecan or walnut
    halves, lightly toasted
125 g/4 oz varied glacé
    cherries
100 g/3½ oz pitted prunes
    or dates
2 tbsp clear honey, to glaze

Preheat the oven to 170°C/325°F/Gas Mark 3, 10 minutes before baking. Heat the butter and sugar in a saucepan until the sugar has dissolved, stirring frequently. Add the pineapple and juice, dried fruits and peel. Bring to the boil, simmer for 3 minutes, stirring occasionally, then remove from the heat to cool completely.

Lightly oil and line the base of a 20.5 x 7.5 cm/8 x 3 inch loose-bottomed cake tin with nonstick baking parchment. Sift the flour, bicarbonate of soda, spices and salt into a bowl. Add the boiled fruit mixture to the flour with the eggs and mix. Spoon into the tin and smooth the top. Bake in the oven for 1¼ hours, or until a skewer inserted into the centre comes out clean. (If the cake is browning too quickly, cover loosely with foil and reduce the oven temperature.)

Remove and cool completely before removing from the tin and discarding the lining paper. Arrange the nuts, cherries and prunes or dates in an attractive pattern on top of the cake. Heat the honey and brush over the topping to glaze. Alternatively, toss the nuts and fruits in the warm honey and spread evenly over the top of the cake.

Cool completely and store in a cake tin for a day or two before serving, to allow the flavours to develop.

Try this: FOR AN ALTERNATIVE: 174   FOR A TEA PARTY: 228

Prize Rosette Cupcakes

MAKES 12

125 g/4 oz self-raising flour
125 g/4 oz caster sugar
125 g/4 oz soft margarine
2 medium eggs, beaten
1 tsp vanilla extract

To decorate:
125 g/4 oz buttercream
  (*see* page 24)
600 g/1 lb 5 oz ready-to-roll
  sugarpaste

red, yellow and blue paste
  food colourings
icing sugar, for dusting
gel writing icing tubes

Preheat the oven to 180°C/350°F/Gas Mark 4, 10 minutes before baking. Line a 12-hole bun tray with paper cases or silicone moulds.

Sift the flour into a bowl and stir together with the caster sugar. Add the margarine, eggs and vanilla extract and beat together for about 2 minutes until smooth.

Spoon the mixture into the cases and bake for 15–20 minutes until golden and firm to the touch. Turn out on a wire rack. When cool, trim the tops flat if they have formed peaks.

To decorate, spread buttercream over the cupcakes and reserve. Break the sugarpaste into three batches and colour each a different colour. Roll out the sugarpaste on a surface lightly dusted with icing sugar and stamp out a fluted circle 6 cm/2½ inches wide with a pastry cutter. Out of the centre of this circle, cut away a small, plain disc 2½ cm/1 inch wide and discard. Take a cocktail stick and roll this back and forth in the sugarpaste icing until it begins to frill up. Take the frilled circle and place in the buttercream, fluting up the edges. Make another fluted circle in a contrasting colour and place this inside the first layer. Stamp out a plain circle and place this in the centre. Write prizes, such as '1st', '2nd' and '3rd', in gel icing in the centres. Keep for 3 days in a cool place in an airtight container.

Try this: FOR AN ALTERNATIVE: 128   FOR A TEA PARTY: 244

Winter Wedding Cupcakes

MAKES 12–14

125 g/4 oz butter
125 g/4 oz soft dark
    muscovado sugar
2 medium eggs, beaten
225 g/8 oz self-raising flour
1 tsp ground mixed spice
finely grated zest and 1 tbsp
    juice from 1 orange

1 tbsp black treacle
350 g/12 oz mixed dried fruit

To decorate:

3 tbsp sieved apricot glaze
    (*see* page 26)
450 g/1 lb almond paste
    (*see* page 26)

icing sugar, for dusting
225 g/8 oz ready-to-roll
    sugarpaste
225 g/8 oz royal icing
fancy paper wrappers
    (optional)

Preheat the oven to 180°C/350°F/Gas Mark 4, 10 minutes before baking. Line one or two 12-hole muffin trays with 12–14 deep paper cases, depending on the depth of the holes.

Beat the butter and sugar together until light and fluffy, then beat in the eggs a little at a time, adding 1 teaspoon flour after each addition. Sift in the remaining flour and the spice, add the orange zest and juice, treacle and dried fruit to the bowl and fold together until the mixture is blended. Spoon into the tins and bake for 30 minutes until firm in the centre and a skewer comes out clean. Leave to cool in the tins for 15 minutes, then turn out onto a wire rack. Store undecorated in an airtight container for up to 3 weeks, or freeze until needed.

To decorate the cupcakes, trim the top of each cake level, then brush with apricot glaze. Roll out the almond paste and cut out eight discs 6 cm/2½ inches wide. Place these over the glaze and press level. Leave to dry for 24 hours if possible.

Dust a clean, flat surface with icing sugar. Roll out the sugarpaste and stamp out holly leaf and ivy shapes. Leave to dry for 2 hours on nonstick baking parchment or clingfilm. Swirl the royal icing over the top of each cupcake. Press in the holly and ivy shapes and leave to set for 2 hours. Once decorated, keep in an airtight container for 3 days.

Hanukkah Honey Spice Cupcakes

MAKES 12–14

1 tsp instant coffee granules
6 tbsp hot water
175 g/6 oz plain flour
1 tsp baking powder
½ tsp bicarbonate of soda
½ tsp ground cinnamon

½ tsp ground ginger
pinch ground cloves
2 medium eggs
125 g/4 oz golden
    caster sugar
175 g/6 oz honey

5 tbsp vegetable oil
50 g/2 oz walnuts,
    finely chopped
125 g/4 oz golden icing
    sugar, to decorate

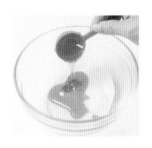

Preheat the oven to 160˚C/325˚F/Gas Mark 3, 10 minutes before baking. Line one or two muffin trays with 12–14 deep paper cases, depending on the depth of the holes. Dissolve the coffee in the water and leave aside to cool.

Sift the flour with the baking powder, bicarbonate of soda and spices. In another bowl, beat the eggs with the sugar and honey until smooth and light, then gradually beat in the oil until blended. Stir this into the flour mixture along with the coffee and walnuts. Beat until smooth.

Carefully spoon the mixture into the paper cases. Fill each halfway up. Take care not to overfill them, as the mixture will rise up. Bake for 25–30 minutes until they are risen, firm and golden. Leave in the tins for 5 minutes, then turn out onto a wire rack to cool.

To decorate, blend the icing sugar with 1 tablespoon warm water to make a thin glacé icing. Place in a paper icing bag and snip away the tip. Pipe large daisies on the top of each cupcake and leave to set for 30 minutes. Keep in an airtight container for up to 5 days.

Try this: FOR AN ALTERNATIVE: 148   FOR A TEA PARTY: 256

Double Chocolate Cake with Cinnamon

SERVES 10

50 g/2 oz cocoa powder
1 tsp ground cinnamon
225 g/8 oz self-raising flour
225 g/8 oz unsalted butter
    or margarine
225 g/8 oz caster sugar
4 large eggs

For the filling:
125 g/4 oz white chocolate
50 ml/2 fl oz double cream
25 g/1 oz dark chocolate

Preheat the oven to 190°C/375°F/Gas Mark 5, 10 minutes before baking. Lightly oil and line the base of two 20.5 cm/8 inch sandwich tins with greaseproof paper or baking parchment. Sift the cocoa powder, cinnamon and flour together and reserve.

In a large bowl, cream the butter or margarine and sugar until light and fluffy. Beat in the eggs a little at a time until they are all incorporated and the mixture is smooth. (If it looks curdled at any point, beat in 1 tablespoon of the sifted flour.)

Using a metal spoon or rubber spatula, fold the sifted flour and cocoa powder into the egg mixture until well mixed. Divide between the two prepared cake tins and level the surface. Bake in the preheated oven for 25–30 minutes until springy to the touch and a skewer inserted into the centre of the cake comes out clean. Turn out onto a wire rack to cool.

To make the filling, roughly break the white chocolate and heat the cream very gently in a small saucepan. Add the broken chocolate, stirring until melted. Leave to cool, then, using half of the cooled white chocolate, sandwich the cakes together.

Top the cake with the remaining cooled white chocolate. Coarsely grate the dark chocolate over the top and serve.

Try this: FOR AN ALTERNATIVE: 168   FOR A TEA PARTY: 198

New Home Cupcakes

MAKES 14

125 g/4 oz self-raising flour
125 g/4 oz caster sugar
125 g/4 oz soft margarine
2 medium eggs, beaten
1 tsp vanilla extract

To decorate:
125 g/4 oz buttercream
  (*see* page 24)
icing sugar, for dusting
450 g/1 lb ready-to-roll
  sugarpaste

yellow, brown and red paste
  food colourings
gel writing icing tubes

Preheat the oven to 180°C/350°F/Gas Mark 4, 10 minutes before baking. Line two 12-hole bun trays with 14 paper fairy-cake cases or silicone moulds.

Sift the flour into a bowl and stir together with the caster sugar. Add the margarine, eggs and vanilla extract and beat together for about 2 minutes until smooth.

Spoon into the cases and bake for 15–20 minutes until golden and firm to the touch. Turn out on a wire rack. When cool, trim the tops flat if they have peaked slightly.

To decorate, lightly coat the top of each cupcake with a little buttercream. Dust a clean, flat surface with icing sugar. Colour half the sugarpaste a pale lemon yellow and roll it out thinly. Cut out circles 6 cm/2½ inches wide and place these over the buttercream and press to smooth down. Colour half the remaining icing brown and the other half red. Roll out thinly on a dusted surface. Cut out small squares in the brown icing and then measure across and cut out a triangular roof shape in red icing. Press the shapes onto the cupcake and pipe on doors, windows and roof tiles in white writing icing. Keep for 3 days in an airtight container.

Try this: FOR AN ALTERNATIVE: 174   FOR A TEA PARTY: 230

Silver Wedding Celebration Cupcakes

MAKES 24

150 g/5 oz butter, softened
150 g/5 oz caster sugar
150 g/5 oz self-raising flour
25 g/1 oz ground almonds
3 medium eggs, beaten
1 tsp almond extract
2 tbsp milk

To decorate:
350 g/12 oz sugarpaste
edible silver dusting powder
450 g/1 lb fondant icing sugar
24 small silver ribbon bows

Preheat the oven to 180°C/350°F/Gas Mark 4, 10 minutes before baking. Line two 12-hole bun trays with silver foil cases.

Place the butter and sugar in a bowl, then sift in the flour and stir in the almonds. Add the beaten eggs to the bowl along with the almond extract and milk and beat until smooth. Spoon into the cases, filling them three-quarters full. Bake for about 18 minutes until firm to the touch in the centre. Turn out onto a wire rack. Once cool, trim the tops of the cupcakes if they have peaked.

To decorate the cupcakes, first line an egg box with foil. Roll the sugarpaste into pea-size balls and mould each one into a petal shape. Mould a cone shape and wrap a petal completely round this. Take another petal and wrap round the first, overlapping. Continue wrapping 4–5 petals round until a rose has formed. Pull the thick base away, flute out the petals and place in the egg box. Repeat until you have 24 roses. Leave them to dry out for 2–4 hours. When they are firm, brush edible silver dust lightly over each rose with a clean paintbrush.

Mix the fondant icing sugar with water, according to the packet instructions, to a thick icing of a spreading consistency. Spread over the top of each cupcake. Work quickly, as this icing will set. Press a rose into the icing and place a thin silver bow on each cupcake. Leave to set for 30 minutes. Keep in a cool place for 2 days. Remove the bows before eating.

Try this: FOR AN ALTERNATIVE: 118   FOR A TEA PARTY: 218

Chocolate Holly Leaf Muffins

MAKES 12

125 g/4 oz caster sugar
125 g/4 oz soft tub
  margarine
2 medium eggs
125 g/4 oz self-raising flour
½ tsp baking powder
50 g/2 oz plain or milk
  chocolate chips

To decorate:
12 holly leaves, washed
  and dried
75 g/3 oz dark chocolate,
  melted
50 g/2 oz unsalted
  butter, softened
300 g/11 oz icing sugar, sifted

125 g/4 oz full-fat
  cream cheese
50 g/2 oz milk chocolate,
  melted and cooled
1 tsp vanilla extract

Preheat the oven to 190°C/375°F/Gas Mark 5, 10 minutes before baking. Line a 12-hole muffin tray with deep paper cases.

Place all the cupcake ingredients except the chocolate chips in a large bowl and beat with an electric mixer for about 2 minutes until smooth. Fold in the chocolate chips, then fill the paper cases halfway up with the mixture. Bake for about 15 minutes until firm, risen and golden. Remove to a wire rack to cool.

To decorate, paint the underside of each holly leaf with the melted dark chocolate. Leave to dry out on nonstick baking parchment for 1 hour, or in the refrigerator for 30 minutes.

Beat the butter until soft, then gradually beat in the icing sugar until light. Add the cream cheese and whisk until fluffy. Divide the mixture in half and beat the cooled melted milk chocolate into one half and the vanilla extract into the other half. Fit a piping bag with a wide star nozzle and spoon the chocolate icing on one side of the bag and the vanilla icing on the other. Pipe swirls on top of the cupcakes.

Peel the holly leaves away from the set chocolate and decorate the top of each cupcake with a chocolate leaf. Keep for 3 days in an airtight container in a cool place.

Try this: FOR AN ALTERNATIVE: 180   FOR A TEA PARTY: 254

Gingerbread

CUTS INTO 8 SLICES

175 g/6 oz butter or
  margarine
225 g/8 oz black treacle
50 g/2 oz dark
  muscovado sugar
350 g/12 oz plain flour

2 tsp ground ginger
150 ml/¼ pint milk, warmed
2 medium eggs
1 tsp bicarbonate of soda
1 piece stem ginger in syrup
1 tbsp stem ginger syrup

Preheat the oven to 150°C/300°F/Gas Mark 2, 10 minutes before baking. Lightly oil and line the base of a 20.5 cm/8 inch, deep, round cake tin with greaseproof paper or baking parchment.

In a saucepan, gently heat the butter or margarine, black treacle and sugar, stirring occasionally, until the butter melts. Leave to cool slightly.

Sift the flour and ground ginger into a large bowl. Make a well in the centre, then pour in the treacle mixture. Reserve 1 tablespoon of the milk, then pour the rest into the treacle mixture. Stir together lightly until mixed.

Beat the eggs together, then stir into the mixture. Dissolve the bicarbonate of soda in the remaining 1 tablespoon of the warmed milk and add to the mixture.

Beat the mixture until well mixed and free of lumps. Pour into the prepared tin and bake in the preheated oven for 1 hour, or until well risen and a skewer inserted into the centre comes out clean.

Cool in the tin, then remove. Slice the stem ginger into thin slivers and sprinkle over the cake. Drizzle with the syrup and serve.

Try this: FOR AN ALTERNATIVE: 166 FOR A TEA PARTY: 248

Pink Candle Cupcakes

MAKES 12

75 g/3 oz fresh raspberries
150 g/5 oz butter, softened
150 g/5 oz caster sugar
175 g/6 oz self-raising flour
3 medium eggs
1 tsp vanilla extract

To decorate:
1 batch cream cheese
  frosting (*see* page 24)
pink liquid food colouring
12 small pink candles

Preheat the oven to 180˚C/350˚F/Gas Mark 4, 10 minutes before baking. Line a 12-hole muffin tray with deep paper cases.

Press the raspberries through a sieve to make a purée. Cream the butter and sugar together in a bowl, then sift in the flour. In another bowl, beat the eggs with the vanilla extract, then add to the butter and sugar mixture. Beat until smooth, then fold in the purée. Spoon into the cases, filling them three-quarters full.

Bake for about 18 minutes until firm to the touch in the centre. Turn out to cool on a wire rack.

Colour the frosting pink with a few drops of food colouring. Place in a piping bag fitted with a star nozzle and pipe large swirls on top of each cupcake. Top each cupcake with a tiny candle. Keep for 3 days in an airtight container in a cool place.

Try this: FOR AN ALTERNATIVE: 128   FOR A TEA PARTY: 188

Easter Nest Cupcakes

MAKES 12

125 g/4 oz soft margarine
125 g/4 oz golden
   caster sugar
150 g/5 oz self-raising flour
2 tbsp cocoa powder
2 medium eggs
1 tbsp golden syrup

To decorate:
1 batch buttercream
  (*see* page 24)
50 g/2 oz shredded
  wheat cereal
125 g/4 oz milk chocolate,
  broken into pieces

25 g/1 oz unsalted butter
chocolate mini eggs

Preheat the oven to 180°C/350°F/Gas Mark 4, 10 minutes before baking. Line a 12-hole bun tray with paper cases.

Place the margarine and the sugar in a large bowl, then sift in the flour and cocoa powder. In another bowl, beat the eggs with the syrup, then add to the first bowl. Whisk together with an electric beater for 2 minutes, or by hand with a wooden spoon until smooth.

Divide the mixture between the cases, filling them three-quarters full. Bake for about 15 minutes until they are springy to the touch in the centre. Turn out to cool on a wire rack.

To decorate, swirl some buttercream over the top of each cupcake. Break up the shredded wheat finely. Melt the chocolate with the butter, then stir in the shredded wheat and let cool slightly. Line a plate with clingfilm. Mould the mixture into tiny nest shapes with your fingers, then place them on the lined plate. Freeze for a few minutes to harden. Set a nest on top of each cupcake and fill with mini eggs. Keep for 2 days in a cool place in an airtight container.

Try this: FOR AN ALTERNATIVE: 184   FOR A TEA PARTY: 244

Hogmanay Party Cupcakes

MAKES 14

125 g/4 oz self-raising flour
125 g/4 oz caster sugar
125 g/4 oz soft margarine
2 medium eggs, beaten
1 tsp vanilla extract

To decorate:
125 g/4 oz buttercream
(*see* page 24)
icing sugar, for dusting
450 g/1 lb ready-to-roll
sugarpaste

yellow, green and lilac paste
food colourings

Preheat the oven to 180°C/350°F/Gas Mark 4, 10 minutes before baking. Line two 12-hole bun trays with 14 paper fairy-cake cases or silicone moulds.

Sift the flour into a bowl and stir together with the caster sugar. Add the margarine and eggs. Beat with the vanilla extract for about 2 minutes until smooth. Spoon into the cases and bake for 15–20 minutes until golden and firm to the touch. Turn out onto a wire rack. When cool, trim the tops flat if they have peaked slightly.

To decorate, lightly coat the top of each fairy cake with a little buttercream. Dust a clean, flat surface with icing sugar. Colour half the sugarpaste a pale cream shade and roll out thinly. Stamp out circles 6 cm/2½ inches wide and place these on the buttercream to cover the top of each fairy cake.

Colour the remaining icing green and lilac. Mould the green icing into stems as pictured or, to be more thistle-like, place a small ball onto each thin stem to form the bulbous part. Mark the bulbous parts of the stems with 'spikes', and position on the fairy cakes. Roll out the lilac sugarpaste into a long, thin strip about 2.5 cm/1 inch wide. Cut with a knife, or snip with scissors, three-quarters of the way through the paste, then roll up to form a tassel for a thistle top and attach to the top of a stem. Repeat on all the cakes. Keep for 3 days in an airtight container.

Chocolate Box Cake

CUTS INTO 16 SLICES

For the chocolate sponge:
175 g/6 oz self-raising flour
1 tsp baking powder
175 g/6 oz caster sugar
175 g/6 oz butter, softened
3 large eggs
25 g/1 oz cocoa powder
150 g/5 oz apricot preserve

For the chocolate box:
275 g/10 oz dark chocolate

For the chocolate whipped cream topping:
450 ml/¾ pint double cream
275 g/10 oz dark chocolate, melted

2 tbsp brandy
1 tsp cocoa powder, to decorate

Preheat the oven to 180°C/350°F/Gas Mark 4, 10 minutes before baking. Lightly oil and flour a 20.5 cm/8 inch square cake tin. Sift the flour and baking powder into a large bowl and stir in the sugar. Using an electric whisk, beat in the butter and eggs. Blend the cocoa powder with 1 tablespoon water, then beat into the creamed mixture. Turn into the tin and bake in the preheated oven for about 25 minutes until well risen and cooked. Remove and cool before removing the cake from the tin.

For the chocolate box, break the chocolate into small pieces, put in a bowl over a saucepan of gently simmering water and leave until soft. Stir occasionally until melted and smooth. Line a Swiss roll tin with nonstick baking parchment and pour in the melted chocolate, tilting the tin to level. Leave until set, then turn out onto a chopping board and carefully strip off the paper. Cut into four strips, the same length as the sponge, using a large, sharp knife that has been dipped into hot water. Gently heat the apricot preserve, sieve to remove lumps and brush over the top and sides of the cake. Carefully place the chocolate strips around the cake sides and press lightly. Leave to set for at least 10 minutes.

For the topping, whisk the cream to soft peaks and quickly fold into the melted chocolate with the brandy. Spoon the chocolate whipped cream into a pastry bag fitted with a star nozzle and pipe a decorative design of rosettes or shells over the surface. Dust with cocoa powder and serve.

Try this: FOR AN ALTERNATIVE: 162 FOR A TEA PARTY: 190

Blue Bow Cupcakes

MAKES 12

150 g/5 oz butter, softened
150 g/5 oz caster sugar
175 g/6 oz self-raising flour
3 medium eggs
1 tsp vanilla extract

To decorate:
1 batch cream cheese
   frosting (*see* page 24)
blue paste food colouring
narrow blue ribbon
cocktail sticks

Preheat the oven to 180°C/350°F/Gas Mark 4, 10 minutes before baking. Line a 12-hole muffin tray with deep paper cases.

Place the butter and sugar in a bowl, then sift in the flour. In another bowl, beat the eggs with the vanilla extract, then add to the bowl. Beat until smooth, then spoon into the cases, filling them three-quarters full.

Bake for about 18 minutes until firm to the touch in the centre. Turn out to cool on a wire rack.

To decorate the cupcakes, colour the frosting with a few drops of blue food colouring. Place in a piping bag fitted with a star nozzle and pipe large swirls on top of each cupcake.

Make tiny bows from the narrow ribbon and slide each one onto a cocktail stick. Top each cupcake with a tiny bow, taking care to keep the ribbon out of the icing.

Keep for 2 days in an airtight container in a cool place. Remember to remove the cocktail sticks and bows before eating the cupcakes

 Try this: FOR AN ALTERNATIVE: 128   FOR A TEA PARTY: 208

Harvest Festival Cupcakes

MAKES 12

175 g/6 oz self-raising
wholemeal flour
1 tsp baking powder
½ tsp ground cinnamon
pinch salt
150 ml/¼ pint
sunflower oil

150 g/5 oz soft light
brown sugar
3 medium eggs, beaten
1 tsp vanilla extract
50 g/2 oz sultanas
225 g/8 oz carrots, peeled
and finely grated

To decorate:
1 batch cream cheese
frosting (*see* page 24)
paste food colourings
225 g/8 oz ready-to-roll
sugarpaste

Preheat the oven to 180°C/350°F/Gas Mark 4, 10 minutes before baking. Lightly oil a deep 12-hole muffin tray or line with deep paper cases.

Sift the flour, baking powder, cinnamon and salt into a bowl, along with any bran from the sieve. Add the oil, sugar, eggs, vanilla extract, sultanas and grated carrots.

Beat until smooth and then spoon into the muffin tray. Bake for 20–25 minutes until risen and golden. Cool on a wire rack.

To decorate, colour the frosting pale green and smooth over the top of each cupcake. Colour the sugarpaste in small batches of orange, red, green and brown and mould into cabbages, carrots, potatoes and tomatoes. Press green sugarpaste through a garlic press to make green carrot leaves. Place the vegetables on top of each cupcake. Keep for 3 days in an airtight container in a cool place.

Try this: FOR AN ALTERNATIVE: 164   FOR A TEA PARTY: 262

Chocolate Chiffon Cake

**CUTS INTO
10–12 SLICES**

50 g/2 oz cocoa powder
300 g/11 oz self-raising flour
550 g/1 lb 3 oz caster sugar
7 medium eggs, separated
125 ml/4 fl oz vegetable oil
1 tsp vanilla extract

200 g/7 oz dark chocolate,
   melted
75 g/3 oz walnuts

For the icing:
175 g/6 oz butter

275 g/10 oz icing sugar,
   sifted
2 tbsp cocoa powder, sifted
2 tbsp brandy

Preheat the oven to 170˚C/325˚F/Gas Mark 3, 10 minutes before baking. Lightly oil and line a 23 cm/9 inch round cake tin. Lightly oil a baking sheet. Blend the cocoa powder with 175 ml/6 fl oz boiling water and leave to cool. Place the flour and 350 g/12 oz of the caster sugar in a large bowl. Add the cocoa mixture, egg yolks, oil and vanilla extract. Whisk until smooth and lighter in colour. Whisk the egg whites in a clean, grease-free bowl until soft peaks form, then fold into the cocoa mixture. Pour into the tin and bake for 1 hour, or until firm. Leave for 5 minutes, then turn out onto a wire rack to cool.

For the icing, cream together 125 g/4 oz of the butter with the icing sugar, cocoa powder and brandy until smooth, then reserve. Melt the remaining butter and blend with 150 g/5 oz of the melted dark chocolate. Stir until smooth and then leave until thickened. Place the remaining caster sugar into a heavy-based saucepan over a low heat and heat until the sugar has melted and is a deep golden brown. Add the walnuts and the remaining melted chocolate to the melted sugar and pour onto the baking sheet. Leave until cold and brittle, then chop finely. Reserve.

Split the cake into three layers. Place one layer onto a plate and spread with half of the brandy butter icing. Top with a second cake layer, spread with the remaining brandy butter icing; arrange the third cake layer on top. Cover the cake with the thickened chocolate glaze. Sprinkle with the walnut praline and serve.

 Try this: FOR AN ALTERNATIVE: 156   FOR A TEA PARTY: 264

Halloween Cobweb Cupcakes

MAKES 16–18

175 g/6 oz caster sugar
175 g/6 oz soft margarine
3 medium eggs, beaten
150 g/5 oz self-raising flour
1 tsp baking powder
25 g/1 oz cocoa powder

To decorate:
225 g/8 oz icing sugar, sifted
2 tbsp warm water
black and orange paste
    food colourings

Preheat the oven to 180°C/350°F/Gas Mark 4, 10 minutes before baking. Line two 12-hole bun trays with 16–18 paper or foil cases, depending on the depth of the holes.

Place the sugar, margarine and eggs in a bowl, then sift in the flour, baking powder and cocoa powder. Beat for 2 minutes or until smooth.

Spoon the mixture into the paper cases and bake for 15–20 minutes until well risen and the tops spring back when lightly pressed. Transfer to a wire rack to cool, then trim the tops of the cupcakes flat if they have any peaks.

To decorate the cupcakes, gradually mix the icing sugar with enough warm water to give a coating consistency. Colour a little of the icing black and place in a small paper icing bag. Colour the remaining icing bright orange.

Work on one cupcake at a time. Spread orange icing over the top of the cupcake. Snip a small hole in the end of the icing bag, then pipe a black spiral on top of the wet orange icing. Use a wooden toothpick and pull this through the icing to give a cobweb effect. Repeat with all the cupcakes and leave to set for 1 hour. Keep for 2 days in an airtight container in a cool place.

Try this: FOR AN ALTERNATIVE: 160   FOR A TEA PARTY: 254

Christmas Pudding Cupcakes

MAKES 14–18

125 g/4 oz butter
125 g/4 oz soft dark
   muscovado sugar
2 medium eggs, beaten
225 g/8 oz self-raising flour
1 tsp ground mixed spice
finely grated zest and
   1 tbsp juice from 1 orange

1 tbsp black treacle
350 g/12 oz mixed dried fruit

To decorate:
3 tbsp sieved apricot glaze
   (*see* page 26)
225 g/8 oz almond paste
   (*see* page 26)

icing sugar, for dusting
450 g/1 lb ready-to-roll
   sugarpaste
brown, yellow, green and
   red paste food colourings

Preheat the oven to 180°C/350°F/Gas Mark 4, 10 minutes before baking. Line one or two 12-hole bun trays with 14–18 foil fairy-cake cases, depending on the depth of the holes.

Beat the butter and sugar together until light and fluffy, then beat in the eggs a little at a time, adding 1 teaspoon flour with each addition. Sift in the remaining flour and the spice, add the orange zest and juice, treacle and dried fruit to the bowl and fold together until the mixture is blended. Spoon into the cases and bake for about 30 minutes until firm in the centre and a skewer comes out clean. Leave to cool in the tins for 15 minutes, then turn out to cool on a wire rack. Store undecorated in an airtight container for up to 4 weeks, or freeze until needed.

To decorate, trim the top of each cake level if they have peaked, then brush with apricot glaze. Roll out the almond paste and cut out circles 6 cm/2½ inches wide. Place a disc on top of each fairy cake and press level. Leave to dry for 24 hours if possible.

Dust a clean, flat surface with icing sugar. Colour half the sugarpaste brown, roll out thinly and cut out circles 6 cm/2½ inches wide. Place on top of the almond paste and press level. Colour the remaining sugarpaste cream or pale yellow, mould into a fluted disc and press on top to represent custard. Colour scraps of sugarpaste green and red and shape into holly leaves and berries. Keep for 1 week in an airtight container.

Try this: FOR AN ALTERNATIVE: 136   FOR A TEA PARTY: 240

Rich Devil's Food Cake

**CUTS INTO
12–16 SLICES**

450 g/1 lb plain flour
1 tbsp bicarbonate of soda
½ tsp salt
75 g/3 oz cocoa powder
300 ml/½ pint milk
150 g/5 oz butter, softened
400 g/14 oz soft dark
  brown sugar

2 tsp vanilla extract
4 large eggs

**For the chocolate
  fudge frosting:**
275 g/10 oz caster sugar
½ tsp salt

125 g/4 oz dark chocolate,
  chopped
225 ml/8 fl oz milk
2 tbsp golden syrup
125 g/4 oz butter, diced
2 tsp vanilla extract

Preheat the oven to 180°C/350°F/Gas Mark 4, 10 minutes before baking. Lightly oil and line the bases of three 23 cm/9 inch cake tins with greaseproof paper. Sift the flour, bicarbonate of soda and salt into a bowl. Sift the cocoa powder into another bowl and gradually whisk in a little of the milk to form a paste. Continue whisking in the milk until smooth.

Beat the butter, sugar and vanilla extract until light and fluffy, then gradually beat in the eggs. Stir in the flour and cocoa mixtures alternately in three or four batches. Divide the mixture evenly among the three tins, smoothing the surfaces evenly. Bake for 25–35 minutes until cooked and firm to the touch. Remove, cool and turn out onto a wire rack. Discard the lining paper.

To make the frosting, put the sugar, salt and chocolate into a heavy-based saucepan and stir in the milk until blended. Add the golden syrup and butter. Bring to the boil over a medium-high heat, stirring to help dissolve the sugar. Boil for 1 minute, stirring constantly. Remove from the heat, stir in the vanilla extract and cool. Whisk until thickened and slightly lighter in colour.

Sandwich the three cake layers together with about a third of the frosting, placing the third cake layer with the flat side up. Transfer the cake to a serving plate and, using a metal palette knife, spread the remaining frosting over the top and sides. Swirl the top to create a decorative effect and serve.

Try this: FOR AN ALTERNATIVE: 140   FOR A TEA PARTY: 198

Mother's Day Rose Cupcakes

MAKES 12

125 g/4 oz caster sugar
125 g/4 oz soft tub
    margarine
2 medium eggs
125 g/4 oz self-raising flour
1 tsp baking powder
1 tsp rosewater

To decorate:
50 g/2 oz ready-to-roll
    sugarpaste
pink paste food colouring
350 g/12 oz fondant
    icing sugar

Preheat the oven to 190°C/375°F/Gas Mark 5, 10 minutes before baking. Line a 12-hole bun tray with paper cases.

Place all the cupcake ingredients in a large bowl and beat with an electric mixer for about 2 minutes until smooth. Fill the paper cases halfway up with the mixture. Bake for about 15 minutes until firm, risen and golden. Remove to a wire rack to cool.

To decorate the cupcakes, first line an egg box with foil and set aside. Colour the sugarpaste with pink paste food colouring. Make a small cone shape, then roll a pea-size piece of sugarpaste into a ball. Flatten out the ball into a petal shape and wrap this round the cone shape. Continue adding more petals to make a rose, then trim the thick base, place in the egg box and leave to dry out for 2 hours.

Blend the fondant icing sugar with a little water to make a thick icing of spreading consistency, then colour this pale pink. Smooth over the top of each cupcake and decorate with the roses immediately. Leave to set for 1 hour. Keep for 1 day in an airtight container.

Try this: FOR AN ALTERNATIVE: 150   FOR A TEA PARTY: 188

Wedding Cake

CUTS INTO 50 SLICES

3 quantities Christmas Cake
   mixture (*see* page 116)
6 tbsp brandy or dark rum
To cover the cakes:
150 ml/10 tbsp sieved

apricot jam, warmed
2.15 kg/4¾ lb almond paste
   (*see* page 26)
2.15 kg/4¾ lb ready-to-roll
   sugarpaste (*see* page 27)

To decorate:
450 g/1 lb ready-to roll
   sugarpaste
450 g/1 lb ready-made royal
   icing (*see* page 25)

Preheat the oven to 150°C/300°F/Gas Mark 2. Grease and treble line a 15 cm/6 inch, a 20 cm/
8 inch and a 25.5 cm/10 inch round cake tin. Divide the mixture between the tins to the same depth.
Bake for 1 hour, then reduce the oven to 140°C/275°F/Gas Mark 1 and bake respectively as follows:
1¼ hours, 2 hours and 3 hours. Test, cool, wrap and store according to the recipe on page 116.

Brush each cake with brandy or rum, reserving 3 tablespoons, then with the jam. Divide the almond
paste into three amounts weighing 350 g/12 oz, 800 g/1¾ lb and 1 kg/2¼ lb. Roll out one third of
the first amount into a disc the size of the top of the small cake and place on top. Roll out the
remaining paste into a strip to cover the sides of the cake, then press on. Cover the remaining cakes
and leave to dry out in a cool place for 2 days. Divide the sugarpaste as per the almond paste. On a
surface dusted with icing sugar, roll out into circles large enough to cover the top and sides of each
cake. Brush the remaining brandy or rum over the almond paste and place the sugarpaste on top.
Smooth down over the cakes and trim the edges neatly. Stack the cakes.

Make 4 small roses for the top, 4 medium for the middle and 4 large for the base: mould a small
cone of sugarpaste, then roll some into a pea-size ball, flatten out into a petal, then wrap this round
the cone. Continue making and wrapping more petals, flute out the edges, then trim away the base
and place the roses in an egg box to dry out and harden for 24 hours. Roll out the trimmings and cut
out 4 small, 4 medium and 4 large leaves, mark on veins with a sharp knife, mould to curve and
leave to dry. Place the royal icing in an icing bag fitted with a No. O plain nozzle and pipe sprig and do
decorations on each tier. Trim the base of each cake with a border of thinly rolled sugarpaste, then
position the roses and leaves and stick in place with a dab of royal icing.

Try this: FOR AN ALTERNATIVE: 144   FOR A TEA PARTY: 234

Giftwrapped Presents Cupcakes

MAKES 12–14

125 g/4 oz butter, softened
125 g/4 oz soft dark
    muscovado sugar
2 medium eggs, beaten
225 g/8 oz self-raising flour
1 tsp ground mixed spice
finely grated zest and 1 tbsp
    juice from 1 orange

1 tbsp black treacle
350 g/12 oz mixed dried fruit

To decorate:
3 tbsp sieved apricot glaze
    (*see* page 26)
icing sugar, for dusting

600 g/1 lb 5 oz ready-to-roll
    sugarpaste
red, blue, green and yellow
    paste food colourings

Preheat the oven to 180°C/350°F/Gas Mark 4, 10 minutes before baking. Line one or two 12-hole muffin trays with 12–14 deep paper cases, depending on the depth of the holes.

Beat the butter and sugar together until light and fluffy, then beat in the eggs a little at a time, adding 1 teaspoon flour with each addition. Sift in the remaining flour and the spice, add the orange zest and juice, treacle and dried fruit to the bowl and fold together until the mixture is blended.

Spoon into the cases and bake for about 30 minutes until firm in the centre and a skewer comes out clean. Leave to cool in the tins for 15 minutes, then turn out to cool on a wire rack. Store undecorated in an airtight container for up to 4 weeks, or freeze until needed.

To decorate, trim the top of each cupcake level if they have peaked, then brush with apricot glaze. Dust a clean, flat surface with icing sugar. Colour the sugarpaste in batches and roll out thinly. Cut out circles 6 cm/2½ inches wide. Place a disc on top of each cupcake and press level. Mould coloured scraps into long, thin sausages and roll these out thinly. Place a contrasting colour across each cupcake and arrange into bows and loops. Leave to dry for 24 hours if possible. Keep for 4 days in an airtight container.

Try this: FOR AN ALTERNATIVE: 166   FOR A TEA PARTY: 230

Cranberry & White Chocolate Cake

SERVES 4

225 g/8 oz butter, softened
250 g/9 oz full-fat soft cheese
150 g/5 oz soft light
   brown sugar
200 g/7 oz caster sugar

grated zest of ½ orange
1 tsp vanilla extract
4 medium eggs
375 g/13 oz plain flour
2 tsp baking powder

200 g/7 oz cranberries,
   thawed if frozen
225 g/8 oz white chocolate,
   roughly chopped
2 tbsp orange juice

Preheat the oven to 180˚C/350˚F/Gas Mark 4, 10 minutes before baking. Lightly oil and flour a 23 cm/9 inch kugelhopf tin or ring tin. Using an electric mixer, cream the butter and cheese with the sugars until light and fluffy. Add the grated orange zest and vanilla extract and beat until smooth, then beat in the eggs, one at a time.

Sift the flour and baking powder together and stir into the creamed mixture, beating well after each addition. Fold in the cranberries and 175 g/6 oz of the white chocolate. Spoon into the prepared tin and bake in the preheated oven for 1 hour, or until firm and a skewer inserted into the centre comes out clean. Cool in the tin before turning out onto a wire rack.

Melt the remaining white chocolate, stir until smooth, then stir in the orange juice and leave to cool until thickened. Transfer the cake to a serving plate and spoon over the white chocolate and orange glaze. Leave to set.

Try this: FOR AN ALTERNATIVE: 124 FOR A TEA PARTY: 252

Sparkly Snowflake Cupcakes

MAKES 24

150 g/5 oz butter, softened
150 g/5 oz caster sugar
150 g/5 oz self-raising flour
25 g/1 oz ground almonds
3 medium eggs, beaten
1 tsp almond extract
1 tbsp milk

To decorate:
icing sugar, for dusting
350 g/12 oz sugarpaste
450 g/1 lb royal icing sugar
edible silver balls

Preheat the oven to 180°C/350°F/Gas Mark 4, 10 minutes before baking. Line two 12-hole bun trays with silver foil cases.

Place the butter and sugar in a bowl, then sift in the flour and stir in the almonds. Add the beaten eggs to the bowl with the almond extract and milk. Spoon into the cases, filling them three-quarters full.

Bake for about 18 minutes until firm to the touch in the centre. Turn out onto a wire rack. Once cool, trim the tops of the cupcakes if they have peaked.

To decorate the cupcakes, dust a clean, flat surface with icing sugar. Roll the sugarpaste thinly and trace round a snowflake pattern. Cut round the shapes and leave them to dry flat on a sheet of nonstick baking parchment for 2 hours until firm.

Make up the royal icing according to the packet instructions to a soft icing that will form peaks. Swirl the icing onto the cupcakes and place a snowflake shape centrally on each one. Decorate with silver balls and leave for 30 minutes to set. Keep for 2 days in an airtight container.

Try this: FOR AN ALTERNATIVE: 182   FOR A TEA PARTY: 228

White Chocolate Christmas Cupcakes

MAKES 12–16

150 g/5 oz butter, softened
150 g/5 oz caster sugar
150 g/5 oz self-raising flour
3 medium eggs, beaten
1 tsp vanilla extract
1 tbsp milk

75 g/3 oz white chocolate, finely grated

To decorate:
250 g/9 oz white chocolate, chopped

16 holly leaves, cleaned and dried
1 batch buttercream (*see* page 24)
icing sugar, for dusting

Preheat the oven to 180°C/350°F/Gas Mark 4, 10 minutes before baking. Line one or two 12-hole bun trays with 12–16 foil cases, depending on the depth of the holes.

Place the butter and sugar in a bowl, then sift in the flour. Add the eggs to the bowl with the vanilla extract and milk and beat until smooth. Fold in the grated white chocolate, then spoon into the cases, filling them three-quarters full.

Bake for about 18 minutes until firm to the touch in the centre. Turn out to cool on a wire rack.

To decorate, melt the white chocolate in a heatproof bowl set over a pan of barely simmering water. Use one third of the melted chocolate to paint the undersides of the holly leaves and leave to set for 30 minutes in the refrigerator. Spread one third of the chocolate out onto a clean plastic board. When almost set, make into curls by pulling a sharp knife through the chocolate at an angle until the chocolate curls away from the knife. Stir the remaining cooled chocolate into the buttercream and chill for 15 minutes.

Swirl each cupcake with buttercream, then press on the white chocolate curls. Peel the holly leaves away from the chocolate and carefully place on top of the cupcakes. Dust with icing sugar before serving. Keep for 2 days in the refrigerator.

Try this: FOR AN ALTERNATIVE: 172 FOR A TEA PARTY: 234

Festive Candy Cane Cupcakes

MAKES 14–18

150 g/5 oz butter, softened
150 g/5 oz caster sugar
150 g/5 oz self-raising flour
25 g/1 oz ground almonds
3 medium eggs, beaten

1 tsp vanilla extract
2 tbsp milk

To decorate:
225 g/8 oz sugarpaste

red and green paste
  food colourings
icing sugar, for dusting
450 g/1 lb royal icing sugar

Preheat the oven to 180°C/350°F/Gas Mark 4, 10 minutes before baking. Line two 12-hole bun trays with 14–18 foil cases, depending on the depth of the holes.

Place the butter and sugar in a bowl, then sift in the flour and stir in the almonds. Add the eggs to the bowl along with the vanilla extract and milk. Spoon into the cases, filling them three-quarters full.

Bake for about 18 minutes until firm to the touch in the centre. Turn out onto a wire rack. Once cool, trim the tops of the cupcakes if they have peaked.

To decorate, colour one quarter of the sugarpaste red and one quarter green. Dust a clean, flat surface with icing sugar. Roll out the sugarpaste into long, very thin sausages with the palms of your hands. Roll a sausage of red or green with a sausage of white to form a twist. Cut into short lengths about 5 cm/2½ inches long and bend round to form a cane shape. Leave to dry out flat for 2 hours until firm.

Make up the royal icing according to the packet instructions to a soft icing that will form peaks. Smooth the icing onto the cupcakes and place a cane centrally on each one. Place the remaining icing in a small piping bag fitted with a star nozzle and pipe a star border round the outside edge of each cupcake. Keep for 2 days in an airtight container.

Try this: FOR AN ALTERNATIVE: 174 FOR A TEA PARTY: 248

Simnel Easter Muffins

MAKES 6–8

125 g/4 oz yellow marzipan
150 ml/¼ pint milk
50 g/2 oz soft light
   brown sugar

2 medium eggs
175 g/6 oz self-raising flour
½ tsp mixed spice
75 g/3 oz mixed dried fruit

50 g/2 oz glacé cherries,
   washed and chopped
75 g/3 oz butter, melted
   and cooled

Preheat the oven to 190°C/375°F/Gas Mark 5, 10 minutes before baking. Line a deep muffin tray with 6–8 paper cases, depending on the depth of the holes. Weigh 25 g/1 oz of the marzipan and roll into long, thin strips. Grate or chop the remaining marzipan into small chunks.

Whisk the milk, sugar and eggs together in a jug. Sift the flour and spice into a bowl, then stir together with the dried fruit, cherries and the marzipan chunks. Pour the milk mixture into the flour mixture along with the melted butter. Mix until combined.

Spoon into the paper cases and make a cross over the top of each using two marzipan strips. Bake in the preheated oven for about 20 minutes until firm in the centre. Cool in the tray for 3 minutes, then turn out to cool on a wire rack. Eat warm or cold. Keep for 24 hours sealed in an airtight container.

Try this: FOR AN ALTERNATIVE: 152   FOR A TEA PARTY: 212

Tea Parties

Rose Petal Cupcakes

MAKES 12

125 g/4 oz self-raising flour
125 g/4 oz butter, softened
125 g/4 oz golden
  caster sugar
2 medium eggs, beaten
1 tbsp rosewater

To decorate:
1 egg white
about 80 small, dry
  rose petals
caster sugar, for dusting
175 g/6 oz icing sugar

1 tbsp glycerine
2 tbsp rosewater
pink food colouring

Preheat the oven to 180°C/350°F/Gas Mark 4, 10 minutes before baking. Line a 12-hole bun tray with foil cases.

Sift the flour into a bowl and add the butter, sugar, eggs and rosewater. Beat for about 2 minutes until smooth, then spoon into the paper cases.

Bake in the centre of the preheated oven for about 14 minutes until well risen and springy in the centre. Transfer to a wire rack to cool. Keep undecorated for up to 2 days in an airtight container.

To decorate, first place a large piece of nonstick baking parchment on a flat surface. Beat the egg white until frothy, then brush thinly over the rose petals. Set the petals on the paper. Dust with caster sugar and leave for 3 hours until dry and sparkling.

Beat the icing sugar with the glycerine and rosewater and add enough colouring to give a pale pink colour. Spread over the top of each cupcake and add a circle of rose petals, working quickly, as the icing will begin to set. Leave for 30 minutes before serving. Eat on the day of decorating.

Try this: FOR AN ALTERNATIVE: 218 FOR A DINNER PARTY: 66

Fudgy & Top Hat Chocolate Buns

MAKES 12

50 g/2 oz self-raising flour
25 g/1 oz cocoa powder
½ tsp baking powder
75 g/3 oz butter, softened
75 g/3 oz soft light
  brown sugar
1 medium egg, lightly beaten
1 tbsp milk

For the fudgy icing:
15 g/½ oz unsalted
  butter, melted
1 tbsp milk
15 g/½ oz cocoa
  powder, sifted
40 g/1½ oz icing
  sugar, sifted

25 g/1 oz dark chocolate,
  coarsely grated

For the top hat filling:
150 ml/¼ pint whipping
  cream
2 tsp orange liqueur
1 tbsp icing sugar, sifted

Preheat the oven to 190°C/375°F/Gas Mark 5, 10 minutes before baking. Sift the flour, cocoa powder and baking powder into a bowl. Add the butter, sugar, egg and milk. Beat for 2–3 minutes until light and fluffy.

Divide the mixture equally between 12 paper cases arranged in a bun tray. Bake on the shelf above the centre in the preheated oven for 15–20 minutes until well risen and firm to the touch. Leave in the bun tray for a few minutes, then transfer to a wire rack and leave to cool completely.

For the fudgy icing, mix together the melted butter, milk, cocoa powder and icing sugar. Place a spoonful of icing on the top of six of the buns, spreading out to a circle with the back of the spoon. Sprinkle with grated chocolate.

To make the top hats, use a sharp knife to cut and remove a circle of sponge, about 3 cm/1¼ inches across from each of the six remaining cakes. Whip the cream, orange liqueur and icing sugar together until soft peaks form.

Spoon the filling into a piping bag fitted with a large star nozzle and pipe a swirl in the centre of each cake. Replace the tops, then dust with the remaining icing sugar and serve with the other buns.

Try this: FOR AN ALTERNATIVE: 198   FOR A DINNER PARTY: 62

Mini Cupcakes

MAKES 24

100 g/3½ oz golden
   caster sugar
100 g/3½ oz butter,
   softened
finely grated zest of ½ lemon
   and 1 tsp juice

2 medium eggs, beaten
100 g/3½ oz self-raising flour

To decorate:
50 g/2 oz unsalted
   butter, softened

1 tsp vanilla extract
125 g/4 oz icing sugar, sifted
1 tbsp milk
paste food colourings
sugar sprinkles

Preheat the oven to 190°C/375°F/Gas Mark 5, 10 minutes before baking. Line a 24-hole mini-muffin tray with mini paper muffin cases.

Put the sugar, butter and lemon zest in a large bowl and beat until light and fluffy. Beat in the eggs a little at a time, adding a teaspoon of flour with each addition. Fold in the rest of the flour and the lemon juice and mix until smooth.

Spoon into the mini muffin cases and bake for about 12 minutes until golden and risen. Transfer to a wire rack to cool.

To make the icing, beat the butter and vanilla extract together until light and fluffy, then gradually beat in the icing sugar and milk until a soft, easy-to-spread consistency has formed. Colour the icing in batches with paste food colourings, then spread over the cold cupcakes with a flat-bladed knife. Decorate with sugar sprinkles. Keep in an airtight container for 2 days.

Try this: FOR AN ALTERNATIVE: 234   FOR A DINNER PARTY: 38

Crunchy–topped Citrus Chocolate Slices

CUTS INTO 12 SLICES

175 g/6 oz butter
175 g/6 oz soft light
   brown sugar
finely grated zest of 1 orange
3 medium eggs,
   lightly beaten

1 tbsp ground almonds
175 g/6 oz self-raising flour
¼ tsp baking powder
125 g/4 oz dark chocolate,
   coarsely grated
2 tsp milk

For the crunchy topping:
125 g/4 oz granulated sugar
juice of 2 limes
juice of 1 orange

Preheat the oven to 170°C/325°F/Gas Mark 3, 10 minutes before baking. Oil and line a 28 x 18 x 2.5 cm/11 x 7 x 1 inch cake tin with nonstick baking parchment. Place the butter, sugar and orange zest into a large bowl and cream together until light and fluffy. Gradually add the eggs, beating after each addition, then beat in the ground almonds.

Sift the flour and baking powder into the creamed mixture. Add the grated chocolate and milk, then gently fold in using a metal spoon. Spoon the mixture into the prepared tin.

Bake on the centre shelf of the preheated oven for 35–40 minutes until well risen and firm to the touch. Leave in the tin for a few minutes to cool slightly. Turn out onto a wire rack and remove the baking parchment.

Meanwhile, to make the crunchy topping, place the sugar with the lime and orange juices in a small jug and stir together. Drizzle the sugar mixture over the hot cake, ensuring the whole surface is covered. Leave until completely cold, then cut into 12 slices and serve.

Try this: FOR AN ALTERNATIVE: 232 FOR A DINNER PARTY: 70

Raspberry Butterfly Cupcakes

MAKES 12–14

125 g/4 oz caster sugar
125 g/4 oz soft tub
  margarine
2 medium eggs

125 g/4 oz self-raising flour
½ tsp baking powder
½ tsp vanilla extract

To decorate:
4 tbsp seedless raspberry jam
12–14 fresh raspberries
icing sugar, for dusting

Preheat the oven to 190°C/375°F/Gas Mark 5, 10 minutes before baking. Line one or two bun trays with 12–14 paper cases, depending on the depth of the holes.

Place all the cupcake ingredients in a large bowl and beat with an electric mixer for about 2 minutes until smooth. Fill the paper cases halfway up with the mixture.

Bake for about 15 minutes until firm, risen and golden. Remove to a wire rack to cool. When cold, cut a small circle out of the top of each cupcake and then cut the circle in half to form wings.

Fill each cupcake with a teaspoon of raspberry jam. Replace the wings at an angle and top each with a fresh raspberry. Dust lightly with icing sugar and serve immediately.

Try this: FOR AN ALTERNATIVE: 258   FOR A DINNER PARTY: 94

Rich Chocolate Cupcakes

MAKES 12

175 g/6 oz self-raising flour
25 g/1 oz cocoa powder
175 g/6 oz soft light
  brown sugar
75 g/3 oz butter, melted
2 medium eggs,
  lightly beaten
1 tsp vanilla extract

40 g/1½ oz maraschino
  cherries, drained and
  chopped

For the chocolate icing:
50 g/2 oz dark chocolate
25 g/1 oz unsalted butter
25 g/1 oz icing sugar, sifted

For the cherry icing:
125 g/4 oz icing sugar
10 g/¼ oz unsalted
  butter, melted
1 tsp syrup from the
  maraschino cherries
3 maraschino cherries,
  halved, to decorate

Preheat the oven to 180°C/350°F/Gas Mark 4, 10 minutes before baking. Line a 12-hole muffin tray or deep bun tray with paper muffin cases. Sift the flour and cocoa powder into a bowl. Stir in the sugar, then add the melted butter, eggs and vanilla extract. Beat together with a wooden spoon for 3 minutes, or until well blended.

Divide half the mixture between six of the paper cases. Dry the cherries thoroughly on absorbent kitchen paper, then fold into the remaining mixture and spoon into the rest of the paper cases.

Bake on the shelf above the centre of the preheated oven for 20 minutes, or until a skewer inserted into the centre of a cake comes out clean. Transfer to a wire rack and leave to cool.

For the chocolate icing, melt the chocolate and butter in a heatproof bowl set over a saucepan of simmering water. Remove from the heat and leave to cool for 3 minutes, stirring occasionally. Stir in the icing sugar. Spoon over the six plain chocolate cakes and leave to set.

For the cherry icing, sift the icing sugar into a bowl and stir in 1 tablespoon boiling water, the butter and the cherry syrup. Spoon the icing over the six remaining cakes, decorate each with a halved cherry and leave to set.

Try this: FOR AN ALTERNATIVE: 190 FOR A DINNER PARTY: 84

Banoffee Cupcakes

MAKES 10–12

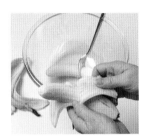

175 g/6 oz soft, ripe bananas
125 g/4 oz soft margarine
75 g/3 oz golden
    caster sugar
1 tbsp milk

2 medium eggs
225 g/8 oz plain flour
1 tbsp baking powder
75 g/3 oz mini soft
    fudge pieces

To decorate:
125 g/4 oz golden
    icing sugar
10–12 semi-dried
    banana flakes

Preheat the oven to 180°C/350°F/Gas Mark 4, 10 minutes before baking. Line a 12-hole muffin tray with 10–12 deep paper cases, depending on the depth of the holes.

Peel and mash the bananas in a large bowl, then add the margarine, sugar, milk and eggs. Sift in the flour and baking powder and beat together for about 2 minutes until smooth.

Fold in 50 g/2 oz of the fudge pieces and then spoon the mixture into the paper cases. Bake for about 20 minutes until golden and firm. Remove from the baking trays to a wire rack to cool.

To decorate, blend the icing sugar with 3–4 teaspoons cold water to make a thin icing. Drizzle over the top of each cupcake and, while the icing is still wet, top with the remaining mini fudge pieces and the banana flakes. Leave to dry out for 30 minutes to set the icing. Keep in an airtight container for 3 days.

Try this: FOR AN ALTERNATIVE: 264   FOR A DINNER PARTY: 98

Chocolate Madeleines

MAKES 10

125 g/4 oz butter
125 g/4 oz soft light
  brown sugar
2 medium eggs,
  lightly beaten
1 drop almond extract
1 tbsp ground almonds
75 g/3 oz self-raising flour

20 g/¾ oz cocoa powder
1 tsp baking powder

To decorate:
5 tbsp apricot conserve
1 tbsp amaretto liqueur,
  brandy or orange juice
50 g/2 oz desiccated coconut

10 large chocolate
  buttons (optional)

Preheat the oven to 180°C/350°F/Gas Mark 4, 10 minutes before baking. Lightly oil 10 dariole moulds and line the bases of each with a small circle of nonstick baking parchment. Stand the moulds on a baking tray. Cream the butter and sugar together until light and fluffy. Gradually add the eggs, beating well after each addition. Beat in the almond extract and ground almonds.

Sift the flour, cocoa powder and baking powder over the creamed mixture. Gently fold in using a metal spoon. Divide the mixture equally between the prepared moulds; each should be about half full.

Bake on the centre shelf of the preheated oven for 20 minutes, or until well risen and firm to the touch. Leave in the tins for a few minutes, then run a small palette knife round the edge and turn out onto a wire rack to cool. Remove the paper circles from the sponges.

Heat the conserve with the liqueur, brandy or juice in a small saucepan. Sieve to remove any lumps. If necessary, trim the sponge bases so they are flat. Brush the tops and sides with warm conserve, then roll in the coconut. Top each with a chocolate button, fixed by brushing its base with conserve.

Try this: FOR AN ALTERNATIVE: 214 FOR A DINNER PARTY: 84

Strawberry Swirl Cupcakes

MAKES 12

125 g/4 oz caster sugar
125 g/4 oz soft tub
  margarine
2 medium eggs
125 g/4 oz self-raising flour
½ tsp baking powder
2 tbsp sieved strawberry jam

To decorate:
50 g/2 oz unsalted butter at
  room temperature
300 g/11 oz icing
  sugar, sifted
125 g/4 oz full-fat
  cream cheese

1 tbsp sieved strawberry jam
pink food colouring

Preheat the oven to 190°C/375°F/Gas Mark 5, 10 minutes before baking. Line a muffin tray with 12 deep paper cases.

Place all the cupcake ingredients except the jam in a large bowl and beat with an electric mixer for about 2 minutes until smooth. Fill the paper cases halfway up with the mixture.

Add ½ teaspoon jam to each case and swirl it into the mixture. Bake for about 15 minutes until firm, risen and golden. Remove to a wire rack to cool.

To prepare the frosting, beat the butter until soft, then gradually add the icing sugar until the mixture is light. Add the cream cheese and whisk until light and fluffy. Divide the mixture in half and beat the strawberry jam and pink food colouring into one half. Fit a piping bag with a wide star nozzle and spoon strawberry cream on one side of the bag and the plain cream on the other. Pipe swirls on top of the cupcakes. Keep for 3 days in an airtight container in a cool place.

Try this: FOR AN ALTERNATIVE: 212   FOR A DINNER PARTY: 108

Moist Mocha & Coconut Cake

MAKES 9

3 tbsp ground coffee
5 tbsp hot milk
75 g/3 oz butter
175 g/6 oz golden syrup
25 g/1 oz soft light
  brown sugar
40 g/1½ oz desiccated
  coconut

150 g/5 oz plain flour
25 g/1 oz cocoa powder
½ tsp bicarbonate of soda
2 medium eggs,
  lightly beaten
3 chocolate flakes,
  to decorate

For the coffee icing:
225 g/8 oz icing sugar, sifted
125 g/4 oz butter, softened

Preheat the oven to 170°C/325°F/Gas Mark 3, 10 minutes before baking. Lightly oil and line a deep, 20.5 cm/8 inch, square tin with nonstick baking parchment. Place the ground coffee in a small bowl and pour over the hot milk. Leave to infuse for 5 minutes, then strain through a tea strainer or a sieve lined with muslin. You will end up with about 4 tablespoons of liquid. Reserve.

Put the butter, golden syrup, sugar and coconut in a small, heavy-based saucepan and heat gently until the butter has melted and the sugar dissolved. Sift the flour, cocoa powder and bicarbonate of soda together and stir into the melted mixture with the eggs and 3 tablespoons of the coffee-infused milk.

Pour the mixture into the prepared tin. Bake on the centre shelf of the preheated oven for 45 minutes, or until the cake is well risen and firm to the touch. Leave in the tin for 10 minutes to cool slightly, then turn out onto a wire rack to cool completely.

For the icing, gradually add the icing sugar to the softened butter and beat together until mixed. Add the remaining 1 tablespoon of the coffee-infused milk and beat until light and fluffy.

Carefully spread the coffee icing over the top of the cake, then cut into nine squares. Decorate each square with a small piece of chocolate flake and serve.

Bluebird Cupcakes

MAKES 12–14

150 g/5 oz butter, softened
150 g/5 oz caster sugar
150 g/5 oz self-raising flour
3 medium eggs, beaten
1 tsp lemon juice
1 tbsp milk

To decorate:
125 g/4 oz sugarpaste
blue paste food colouring
icing sugar, for dusting
1 batch cream cheese
   frosting (*see* page 24)
white gel icing tube

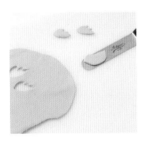

Preheat the oven to 180°C/350°F/Gas Mark 4, 10 minutes before baking. Line a 12-hole muffin tray with 12–14 deep paper cases, depending on the depth of the holes.

Place the butter and sugar in a bowl, then sift in the flour. Add the eggs to the bowl with the lemon juice and milk and beat until smooth. Spoon into the cases, filling them three quarters full.

Bake for about 18 minutes until firm to the touch in the centre. Turn out to cool on a wire rack.

To decorate the cupcakes, colour the sugarpaste blue. Dust a clean, flat surface with icing sugar. Roll out the sugarpaste thinly and mark out bird wings in sets of two and one body per bird. Then stamp out some daisy shapes. Leave all these to dry out for 30 minutes until firm enough to handle.

Swirl some frosting onto each cupcake. Press one bird's body and pair of wings, and some flowers, onto the frosting and pipe on decorations with the white gel icing tubes. Keep in an airtight container in a cool place for 3 days.

Try this: FOR AN ALTERNATIVE: 222   FOR A DINNER PARTY: 110

Lemon–iced Ginger Squares

MAKES 12

225 g/8 oz caster sugar
50 g/2 oz butter, melted
2 tbsp black treacle
2 medium egg whites,
   lightly whisked

225 g/8 oz plain flour
1 tsp bicarbonate of soda
½ tsp ground cloves
1 tsp ground cinnamon
¼ tsp ground ginger

pinch salt
225 ml/8 fl oz buttermilk
175 g/6 oz icing sugar
lemon juice

Preheat the oven to 200°C/400°F/Gas Mark 6, 15 minutes before baking. Lightly oil a 20.5 cm/8 inch square cake tin and sprinkle with a little flour.

Mix together the caster sugar, butter and treacle. Stir in the egg whites.

Mix together the flour, bicarbonate of soda, cloves, cinnamon, ginger and salt.

Stir the flour mixture and buttermilk alternately into the butter mixture until well blended.

Spoon into the prepared tin and bake in the preheated oven for 35 minutes, or until a skewer inserted into the centre of the cake comes out clean.

Remove from the oven and allow to cool for 5 minutes in the tin before turning out onto a wire rack over a large plate. Using a cocktail stick, make holes in the top of the cake.

Meanwhile, mix together the icing sugar with enough lemon juice to make a smooth, pourable icing.

Carefully pour the icing over the hot cake, then leave until cold. Cut the ginger cake into squares and serve.

Try this: FOR AN ALTERNATIVE: 194   FOR A DINNER PARTY: 42

**MAKES 12 LARGE
CUPCAKES OR
18 FAIRY CAKES**

Double Cherry Cupcakes

50 g/2 oz glacé
  cherries, washed,
  dried and chopped
125 g/4 oz self-raising flour
25 g/1 oz dried morello
  cherries

125 g/4 oz soft margarine
125 g/4 oz caster sugar
2 medium eggs
½ tsp almond extract

To decorate:
125 g/4 oz fondant
  icing sugar
pale pink liquid food
  colouring
40 g/1½ oz glacé cherries

Preheat the oven to 190°C/375°F/Gas Mark 5, 10 minutes before baking. Line a 12-hole muffin tray with deep paper cases, or two trays with 18 fairy-cake cases.

Dust the chopped glacé cherries lightly in a tablespoon of the flour, then mix with the morello cherries and reserve. Sift the rest of the flour into a bowl, then add the margarine, sugar, eggs and almond extract. Beat for about 2 minutes until smooth, then fold in the cherries.

Spoon the mixture into the paper cases and bake for 15–20 minutes until well risen and springy in the centre. Turn out to cool on a wire rack.

To decorate the cupcakes, trim the tops level. Mix the icing sugar with 2–3 teaspoons warm water and a few drops pink food colouring to make a thick consistency. Spoon the icing over each cupcake, filling right up to the edge. Chop the cherries finely and sprinkle over the icing. Leave to set for 30 minutes. Keep for 3 days in an airtight container.

Try this: FOR AN ALTERNATIVE: 240   FOR A DINNER PARTY: 64

Chocolate & Coconut Cake

8 SLICES

125 g/4 oz dark chocolate, roughly chopped
175 g/6 oz butter or margarine
175 g/6 oz caster sugar
3 medium eggs, beaten
175 g/6 oz self-raising flour

1 tbsp cocoa powder
50 g/2 oz desiccated coconut

For the icing:
125 g/4 oz butter or margarine
2 tbsp creamed coconut

225 g/8 oz icing sugar
25 g/1 oz desiccated coconut, lightly toasted

Preheat the oven to 180°C/350°F/Gas Mark 4, 10 minutes before baking. Melt the chocolate in a small bowl placed over a saucepan of gently simmering water, ensuring that the base of the bowl does not touch the water. When the chocolate has melted, stir until smooth and allow to cool.

Lightly oil and line the bases of two 18 cm/7 inch sandwich tins with greaseproof or baking paper. In a large bowl, beat the butter or margarine and sugar together with a wooden spoon until light and creamy. Beat in the eggs a little at a time, then stir in the melted chocolate.

Sift the flour and cocoa powder together and gently fold into the chocolate mixture with a metal spoon or rubber spatula. Add the desiccated coconut and mix lightly. Divide between the two prepared tins and smooth the tops.

Bake in the preheated oven for 25–30 minutes until a skewer comes out clean when inserted into the centre of the cake. Allow to cool in the tin for 5 minutes, then turn out, discard the lining paper and leave on a wire rack until cold.

Beat together the butter or margarine and creamed coconut until light. Add the icing sugar and mix well. Spread half the icing on one cake and press the cakes together. Spread the remaining icing over the top, sprinkle with the coconut and serve.

Try this: FOR AN ALTERNATIVE: 260   FOR A DINNER PARTY: 112

Sunflower Cupcakes

MAKES 18

150 g/5 oz butter, softened
150 g/5 oz caster sugar
3 medium eggs, beaten
150 g/5 oz self-raising flour
½ tsp baking powder
zest and 2 tbsp juice from 1
    small orange

To decorate:
1 batch buttercream
    (*see* page 24)
yellow and orange
    food colourings

Preheat the oven to 180°C/350°F/Gas Mark 4, 10 minutes before baking and line two bun trays with 18 paper fairy-cake cases.

Place the butter, sugar and beaten eggs in a bowl, then sift in the flour and baking powder. Finely grate the zest from the orange into the bowl and squeeze out 2 tablespoons juice.

Beat together for about 2 minutes, preferably with an electric hand mixer, until pale and fluffy. Spoon the mixture into the paper cases and bake for about 15 minutes until firm and golden. Cool on a wire rack.

To decorate, colour three quarters of the buttercream bright yellow and the remainder orange. Place in two piping bags fitted with star nozzles. Pipe a border of straight lines round the outer edges to form petals. Pipe more petals to fill in the centres. Pipe a circle of orange dots in the centre of each to finish. Keep for 3 days in a cool place.

Try this: FOR AN ALTERNATIVE: 244 FOR A DINNER PARTY: 96

Crystallised Violet Cupcakes

MAKES 12

150 g/5 oz butter, softened
150 g/5 oz caster sugar
3 medium eggs, beaten
150 g/5 oz self-raising flour
½ tsp baking powder
1 lemon

To decorate:
12 fresh violets
1 egg white
caster sugar, for dusting
125 g/4 oz fondant icing sugar
pale violet food colouring

Preheat the oven to 180°C/350°F/Gas Mark 4, 10 minutes before baking and line a 12-hole muffin tray with deep paper cases.

Place the butter, sugar and eggs in a bowl. Sift in the flour and baking powder. Finely grate in the zest from the lemon.

Beat together for about 2 minutes with an electric hand mixer until pale and fluffy. Spoon into the paper cases and bake for 20–25 minutes until firm and golden. Cool on a wire rack.

To decorate the cupcakes, spread the violets on some nonstick baking parchment. Beat the egg white until frothy, then brush thinly over the violets. Dust with caster sugar and leave to dry out for 2 hours. Beat the icing sugar with the colouring and enough water to give a thin coating consistency. Drizzle over the top of each cupcake quickly and top with a violet. Leave to set for 30 minutes. Store in an airtight container in a cool place. Keep for 2 days.

Try this: FOR AN ALTERNATIVE: 188   FOR A DINNER PARTY: 36

Victoria Sponge with Mango & Mascarpone

CUTS INTO 8 SLICES

175 g/6 oz caster sugar, plus
   extra for dusting
175 g/6 oz self-raising flour,
   plus extra for dusting
175 g/6 oz butter or
   margarine

3 large eggs
1 tsp vanilla extract

For the filling and icing:
25 g/1 oz icing sugar
250 g/9 oz mascarpone
   cheese
1 large, ripe mango, peeled

Preheat the oven to 190°C/375°F/Gas Mark 5, 10 minutes before baking. Lightly oil two 18 cm/7 inch sandwich tins and lightly dust with caster sugar and flour, tapping the tins to remove any excess.

In a large bowl, cream the butter or margarine and sugar together with a wooden spoon until light and creamy. In another bowl, mix the eggs and vanilla extract together. Sift the flour several times onto a plate. Beat a little egg into the butter and sugar, then a little flour, and beat well.

Continue adding the flour and eggs alternately, beating after each addition, until the mixture is well mixed and smooth. Divide between the two cake tins, level the surface, then, using the back of a large spoon, make a slight dip in the centre of each cake.

Bake in the preheated oven for 25–30 minutes until the centre of the cake springs back when gently pressed with a clean finger. Turn out onto a wire rack and leave the cakes until cold.

Beat the icing sugar and mascarpone cheese together, then chop the mango into small cubes. Use half the mascarpone and mango to sandwich the cakes together. Spread the rest of the mascarpone on top, decorate with the remaining mango and serve. Otherwise, lightly cover and store in the refrigerator for 3–4 days.

Try this: FOR AN ALTERNATIVE: 270 FOR A DINNER PARTY: 40

Pink Flower Cupcakes

MAKES 12

150 g/5 oz butter, softened
150 g/5 oz caster sugar
3 medium eggs, beaten
1 tsp vanilla extract
150 g/5 oz self-raising flour
½ tsp baking powder

To decorate:
pink paste food colouring
650 g/1 lb 7 oz ready-to-roll
    sugarpaste
icing sugar, for dusting
½ batch cream cheese
    frosting (*see* page 24)

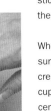

Preheat the oven to 180°C/350°F/Gas Mark 4, 10 minutes before baking and line a 12-hole muffin tray with deep paper cases.

Place the butter, sugar, eggs and vanilla extract in a bowl, then sift in the flour and baking powder. Beat together for about 2 minutes with an electric hand mixer until pale and fluffy. Spoon into the paper cases and bake for 20–25 minutes until firm and golden. Cool on a wire rack.

To decorate the cupcakes, first line a 12-hole egg box with foil. Colour 175 g/6 oz of the sugarpaste pink. Roll it out thinly and, using a cutter, cut out 12 flower shapes. Use a cocktail stick to mark ridges on the petals and mould the icing in your hand to form flower shapes, then leave in the foil-lined egg box for 2 hours.

When the flowers are nearly hardened, roll out the remaining white sugarpaste thinly on a surface dusted with icing sugar and cut out circles 6 cm/2½ inches wide. Spread half the cream cheese frosting thinly over each cupcake and top with a sugarpaste disc. Top each cupcake with a flower, pressing it gently to fix, and pipe a little frosting into the centre of each flower. Keep in a sealed container in a cool place for up to 2 days.

Daisy Chain Lemon Cupcakes

MAKES 12

125 g/4 oz caster sugar
125 g/4 oz soft tub
  margarine
2 medium eggs
125 g/4 oz self-raising flour
½ tsp baking powder
1 tsp lemon juice

To decorate:
50 g/2 oz ready-to-roll
  sugarpaste
yellow piping icing tube
225 g/8 oz fondant
  icing sugar
lemon yellow food colouring

Preheat the oven to 190°C/375°F/Gas Mark 5, 10 minutes before baking. Line a bun tray with 12 paper cases.

Place all the cupcake ingredients in a large bowl and beat with an electric mixer for about 2 minutes until smooth. Fill the paper cases halfway up with the mixture.

Bake for about 15 minutes until firm, risen and golden. Remove to a wire rack to cool.

Roll out the icing thinly and stamp out small daisies with a fluted daisy cutter. Pipe a small yellow dot of icing into the centre of each and leave to dry out for 1 hour. Blend the fondant icing sugar with a little water and a few dots of yellow colouring to make a thick, easy-to-spread icing, then smooth over the top of each cupcake. Decorate with the cut-out daisies immediately and leave to set for 1 hour. Keep for 3 days in an airtight container.

Try this: FOR AN ALTERNATIVE: 216   FOR A DINNER PARTY: 110

Coffee & Pecan Cake

CUTS INTO 8 SLICES

175 g/6 oz self-raising flour
125 g/4 oz butter or
    margarine
175 g/6 oz golden
    caster sugar
1 tbsp instant coffee powder
    or granules

2 large eggs
50 g/2 oz pecans, roughly
    chopped

For the icing:
1 tsp instant coffee powder
    or granules

1 tsp cocoa powder
75 g/3 oz unsalted butter,
    softened
175 g/6 oz icing sugar, sifted
whole pecans, to decorate

Preheat the oven to 190°C/375°F/Gas Mark 5, 10 minutes before baking. Lightly oil and line the bases of two 18 cm/7 inch sandwich tins with greaseproof paper or baking parchment. Sift the flour and reserve.

Beat the butter or margarine and sugar together until light and creamy. Dissolve the coffee in 2 tablespoons hot water and allow to cool.

Lightly mix the eggs with the coffee liquid. Gradually beat into the creamed butter and sugar, adding a little of the sifted flour with each addition.

Fold in the pecans, then divide the mixture between the prepared tins and bake in the preheated oven for 20–25 minutes until well risen and firm to the touch. Leave to cool in the tins for 5 minutes before turning out and cooling on a wire rack.

To make the icing, blend together the coffee and cocoa powder with enough boiling water to make a stiff paste. Beat into the butter and icing sugar. Sandwich the two cakes together using half of the icing. Spread the remaining icing over the top of the cake and decorate with the whole pecans to serve. Store in an airtight container.

Try this: FOR AN ALTERNATIVE: 264   FOR A DINNER PARTY: 90

Florentine–topped Cupcakes

MAKES 18

150 g/5 oz butter, softened
150 g/5 oz caster sugar
175 g/6 oz self-raising flour
3 medium eggs
1 tsp vanilla extract
75 g/3 oz glacé cherries,
    chopped

50 g/2 oz angelica, chopped
50 g/2 oz candied peel,
    chopped
50 g/2 oz dried cranberries

To decorate:
75 g/3 oz plain or milk
    chocolate, melted
50 g/2 oz flaked almonds

Preheat the oven to 180°C/350°F/Gas Mark 4, 10 minutes before baking. Line two 12-hole muffin trays with 18 paper cases.

Place the butter and sugar in a bowl, then sift in the flour. In another bowl, beat the eggs with the vanilla extract, then add to the first mixture and beat until smooth. Fold in half the cherries, angelica, peel and cranberries. Spoon into the cases, filling them three-quarters full.

Bake for about 18 minutes until firm to the touch in the centre. Turn out to cool on a wire rack.

Spoon a little melted chocolate on top of each cupcake, then scatter the remaining cherries, angelica, peel and cranberries and the almonds into the wet chocolate. Drizzle the remaining chocolate over the fruit topping with a teaspoon and leave to set for 30 minutes. Keep for 2 days in an airtight container.

Try this: FOR AN ALTERNATIVE: 212   FOR A DINNER PARTY: 72

Fondant Fancies

MAKES 16–18

150 g/5 oz self-raising flour
150 g/5 oz caster sugar
50 g/2 oz ground almonds
150 g/5 oz butter, softened
3 medium eggs, beaten
4 tbsp milk

To decorate:
450 g/1 lb fondant
icing sugar
paste food colourings
selection fancy cake
decorations

Preheat the oven to 180°C/350°F/Gas Mark 4, 10 minutes before baking. Line two 12-hole bun trays with 16–18 paper cases, depending on the depth of the holes.

Sift the flour into a bowl and stir in the caster sugar and almonds. Add the butter, eggs and milk and beat until smooth.

Spoon into the paper cases and bake for 15–20 minutes until golden and firm to the touch. Turn out to cool on a wire rack. When cool, trim the tops flat if they have peaked slightly.

To decorate the cupcakes, make the fondant icing to a thick coating consistency, following the packet instructions. Divide into batches and colour each separately with a little paste food colouring. Keep each bowl covered with a damp cloth until needed. Spoon some icing over each cupcake, being sure to flood it right to the edge. Top each with a fancy decoration and leave to set for 30 minutes. Keep for 2 days in a cool place.

Try this: FOR AN ALTERNATIVE: 234   FOR A DINNER PARTY: 52

Lemon Drizzle Cake

CUTS INTO 16 SLICES

125 g/4 oz butter or
   margarine
175 g/6 oz caster sugar
2 large eggs

175 g/6 oz self-raising flour
2 lemons, preferably
   unwaxed
50 g/2 oz granulated sugar

Preheat the oven to 180°C/350°F/Gas Mark 4, 10 minutes before baking. Lightly oil and line the base of an 18 cm/7 inch square cake tin with baking parchment.

In a large bowl, cream the butter or margarine and sugar together until soft and fluffy. Beat the eggs, then gradually add a little of the egg to the creamed mixture, adding 1 tablespoon of the flour after each addition.

Finely grate the zest from one of the lemons and stir into the creamed mixture, beating well until smooth. Squeeze the juice from the lemon, strain, then stir into the mixture.

Spoon into the tin, level the surface and bake in the oven for 25–30 minutes. Using a zester, remove the peel from the second lemon and mix with 25 g/1 oz of the granulated sugar. Reserve.

Squeeze the juice into a small saucepan. Add the rest of the granulated sugar to the lemon juice in the saucepan and heat gently, stirring occasionally. When the sugar has dissolved, simmer gently for 3–4 minutes until syrupy.

With a cocktail stick or fine skewer, prick the cake all over. Sprinkle the lemon zest and sugar over the top of the cake, drizzle over the syrup and leave to cool in the tin. Cut the cake into squares and serve.

Try this: FOR AN ALTERNATIVE: 210   FOR A DINNER PARTY: 108

Quilted Cupcakes

MAKES 12–14

125 g/4 oz self-raising flour
125 g/4 oz caster sugar
125 g/4 oz soft margarine
2 medium eggs, beaten
1 tsp lemon juice

To decorate:
125 g/4 oz buttercream
  (*see* page 24)
icing sugar, for dusting
450 g/1 lb ready-to-roll
  sugarpaste
edible gold or silver balls

Preheat the oven to 180°C/350°F/Gas Mark 4, 10 minutes before baking. Line two 12-hole bun trays with 12–14 foil cases, depending on the depth of the holes.

Sift the flour into a bowl and stir together with the caster sugar. Add the margarine and eggs and beat together with the lemon juice for about 2 minutes until smooth.

Spoon into the cases and bake in the preheated oven for 15–20 minutes until golden and firm to the touch. Turn out on a wire rack. When cool, trim the tops flat if they have peaked slightly.

To decorate, lightly coat the top of each cupcake with a little buttercream. Dust a clean, flat surface with icing sugar. Roll out the sugarpaste and stamp out circles 6 cm/2½ inches wide. Place these on the buttercream to cover the top of each cupcake.

Take a palette knife and press lines into the icing, then mark across in the opposite direction to make small squares. Place an edible gold or silver ball into the corner of each square. Keep for 3 days in an airtight container in a cool place.

Try this: FOR AN ALTERNATIVE: 208 FOR A DINNER PARTY: 58

Toffee Apple Cake

CUTS INTO 8 SLICES

2 small eating apples, peeled
4 tbsp soft dark brown sugar
175 g/6 oz butter or
 margarine
175 g/6 oz caster sugar
3 medium eggs

175 g/6 oz self-raising flour
150 ml/¼ pint double cream
2 tbsp icing sugar
½ tsp vanilla extract
½ tsp ground cinnamon

Preheat the oven to 180°C/350°F/Gas Mark 4, 10 minutes before baking. Lightly oil and line the bases of two 20.5 cm/8 inch sandwich tins with greaseproof paper or baking parchment.

Thinly slice the apples and toss in the brown sugar until well coated. Arrange them over the bases of the prepared tins and reserve.

Cream together the butter or margarine and caster sugar until light and fluffy.

Beat the eggs together in a small bowl and gradually beat them into the creamed mixture, beating well after each addition. Sift the flour into the mixture and, using a metal spoon or rubber spatula, fold in.

Divide the mixture between the two cake tins and level the surfaces. Bake in the preheated oven for 25–30 minutes until golden and well risen. Leave in the tins to cool.

Lightly whip the cream with 1 tablespoon of the icing sugar and the vanilla extract.

Sandwich the cakes together with the cream. Mix the remaining icing sugar and the ground cinnamon together, sprinkle over the top of the cake and serve.

Try this: FOR AN ALTERNATIVE: 256 FOR A DINNER PARTY: 68

Hearts & Flowers Cupcakes

MAKES 12

150 g/5 oz butter, softened
150 g/5 oz caster sugar
175 g/6 oz self-raising flour
3 medium eggs, beaten
1 tsp lemon juice
1 tbsp milk

To decorate:
350 g/12 oz sugarpaste
paste food colourings
icing sugar, for dusting
1 batch cream cheese
    frosting (*see* page 24)

Preheat the oven to 180°C/350°F/Gas Mark 4, 10 minutes before baking. Line a 12-hole muffin tray with deep paper cases.

Place the butter and sugar in a bowl, then sift in the flour. Add the beaten eggs to the bowl with the lemon juice and milk and beat until smooth. Spoon into the cases, filling them three-quarters full.

Bake in the preheated oven for about 18 minutes until firm to the touch in the centre. Turn out to cool on a wire rack.

To decorate, colour the sugarpaste in batches in any colours you like. Dust a clean, flat surface with icing sugar. Roll out the sugarpaste thinly and stamp out daisies using a flower stamp (*see also* page 126), then roll out some more sugarpaste thinly and cut out small heart shapes. Leave these to dry out for 30 minutes until firm enough to handle.

Place the frosting in a piping bag fitted with a star nozzle. Pipe swirls onto each cupcake. Press the flowers and hearts onto the frosting. Keep in an airtight container in a cool place for 3 days.

Try this: FOR AN ALTERNATIVE: 224   FOR A DINNER PARTY: 94

Black Forest Cupcakes

**MAKES 12 LARGE
CUPCAKES OR 24
SMALL CUPCAKES**

1 tbsp cocoa powder
2 tbsp boiling water
175 g/6 oz self-raising flour
1 tsp baking powder
125 g/4 oz soft tub
    margarine
175 g/6 oz soft dark
    brown sugar

2 medium eggs
3 tbsp milk

To decorate:
125 g/4 oz dark chocolate
4 tbsp seedless raspberry
    jam, warmed
150 ml/¼ pint double cream

1 tbsp kirsch (optional)
12 natural-coloured
    glacé cherries

Preheat the oven to 180°C/350°F/Gas Mark 4, 10 minutes before baking. Line a 12-hole muffin tray with large paper cases, or one or two bun trays with 24 small paper cases. Blend the cocoa powder with the boiling water and leave to cool.

Sift the flour and baking powder into a bowl and add the margarine, sugar, eggs, milk and the cocoa mixture. Whisk together for about 2 minutes until smooth, then spoon into the paper cases.

Bake in the preheated oven for 15–20 minutes until springy to the touch. Cool in the tins for 5 minutes, then turn out onto a wire rack to cool.

To decorate, melt the chocolate and spread it out to cool on a clean plastic board. When it is almost set, pull a sharp knife through the chocolate to make curls. Refrigerate these until needed. Brush the top of each cupcake with a little raspberry jam. Whisk the cream until it forms soft peaks, then fold in the kirsch, if using. Pipe or swirl the cream on top of each cupcake. Top with chocolate curls and whole glacé cherries for the large muffins or halved cherries for the smaller ones. Eat fresh or keep for 1 day in the refrigerator.

Try this: FOR AN ALTERNATIVE: 196 FOR A DINNER PARTY: 106

Cappuccino Cupcakes

MAKES 6

125 g/4 oz butter or
  margarine
125 g/4 oz caster sugar
2 medium eggs
1 tbsp strong black coffee
150 g/5 oz self-raising flour

125 g/4 oz mascarpone
  cheese
1 tbsp icing sugar, sifted
1 tsp vanilla extract
cocoa powder, sifted, for
  dusting

Preheat the oven to 190°C/375°F/Gas Mark 5, 10 minutes before baking. Place six large paper muffin cases into a muffin tray or alternatively place onto a baking sheet.

Cream the butter or margarine and sugar together until light and fluffy. Break the eggs into a small bowl and beat lightly with a fork.

Using a wooden spoon, beat the eggs into the butter and sugar mixture a little at a time, until they are all incorporated. If the mixture looks curdled, beat in a spoonful of the flour to return the mixture to a smooth consistency. Finally, beat in the black coffee.

Sift the flour into the mixture, then, with a metal spoon or rubber spatula gently fold in the flour. Place spoonfuls of the mixture into the muffin cases. Bake in the preheated oven for 20–25 minutes until risen and springy to the touch. Cool on a wire rack.

In a small bowl, beat together the mascarpone cheese, icing sugar and vanilla extract. When the cakes are cold, spoon the vanilla mascarpone onto the top of each one. Dust with cocoa powder and serve. Eat within 24 hours and store in the refrigerator.

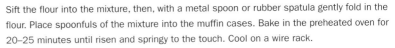

Try this: FOR AN ALTERNATIVE: 250   FOR A DINNER PARTY: 78

Spring Daffodil Cupcakes

MAKES 14

125 g/4 oz self-raising flour
125 g/4 oz caster sugar
125 g/4 oz soft margarine
2 medium eggs, beaten
1 tsp vanilla extract

To decorate:
125 g/4 oz buttercream
   (*see* page 24)
450 g/1 lb ready-to-roll
   sugarpaste

green, yellow and orange
paste food colouring

Preheat the oven to 180°C/350°F/Gas Mark 4, 10 minutes before baking. Line two 12-hole bun trays with 14 paper fairy-cake cases or silicone moulds.

Sift the flour into a bowl and stir together with the caster sugar. Add the margarine, eggs and vanilla extract and beat together for about 2 minutes until smooth.

Spoon into the paper cases and bake for 15–20 minutes until golden and firm to the touch. Turn out onto a wire rack. When cool, trim the tops flat if they have peaked slightly.

To decorate the cupcakes, lightly coat the top of each with a little buttercream. Dust a clean, flat surface with icing sugar. Colour half the sugarpaste light green and roll out thinly. Stamp out circles 6 cm/2½ inches wide and place these on the buttercream to cover the top of each cupcake.

Colour three quarters of the remaining icing yellow and a quarter orange. Roll out the yellow icing on some baking parchment and mark out thin petal shapes. Take six petals and pinch each one together. Place these on the green icing in a circle, then mould a piece of orange icing into a pea-size ball. Mould this into a cone shape and place in the centre of the flower. Keep for 3 days in an airtight container.

Try this: FOR AN ALTERNATIVE: 230   FOR A DINNER PARTY: 70

Whisked Sponge Cake

CUTS INTO 6 SLICES

125 g/4 oz plain flour,
   plus 1 tsp
175 g/6 oz caster sugar,
   plus 1 tsp
3 medium eggs

1 tsp vanilla extract
4 tbsp raspberry jam
50 g/2 oz fresh raspberries,
   crushed
icing sugar, for dredging

Preheat the oven to 200°C/400°F/Gas Mark 6, 15 minutes before baking. Mix 1 teaspoon of the flour and 1 teaspoon of the sugar together. Lightly oil two 18 cm/7 inch sandwich tins and dust lightly with the sugar and flour.

Place the eggs in a large, heatproof bowl. Add the sugar, then place over a saucepan of gently simmering water, ensuring that the base of the bowl does not touch the hot water. Using an electric whisk, beat the sugar and eggs until they become light and fluffy. (The whisk should leave a trail in the mixture when it is lifted out.)

Remove the bowl from the saucepan of water, add the vanilla extract and continue beating for 2–3 minutes. Sift the flour gently into the egg mixture and, using a metal spoon or rubber spatula, carefully fold in, taking care not to overmix and remove all the air that has been whisked in.

Divide the mixture between the two prepared cake tins. Tap lightly on the work surface to remove any air bubbles. Bake in the preheated oven for 20–25 minutes until golden. Test that the cake is ready by gently pressing the centre with a clean finger – it should spring back.

Leave to cool in the tins for 5 minutes, then turn out on to a wire rack. Blend the jam and the crushed raspberries together. When the cakes are cold, spread over the jam mixture and sandwich together. Dredge the top with icing sugar and serve.

Try this: FOR AN ALTERNATIVE: 258   FOR A DINNER PARTY: 86

Gingerbread Cupcakes

MAKES 14–16

8 tbsp golden syrup
125 g/4 oz block margarine
225 g/8 oz plain flour
2 tsp ground ginger

75 g/3 oz sultanas
50 g/2 oz soft dark
brown sugar
175 ml/6 fl oz milk

1 tsp bicarbonate of soda
1 medium egg, beaten
125 g/4 oz golden icing
sugar, to decorate

Preheat the oven to 180°C/350°F/Gas Mark 4, 10 minutes before baking. Line one or two muffin trays with 14–16 deep paper cases, depending on the depth of the holes.

Place the syrup and margarine in a heavy-based pan and melt together gently. Sift the flour and ginger into a bowl, then stir in the sultanas and sugar.

Warm the milk and stir in the bicarbonate of soda. Pour the syrup mixture, the milk and beaten egg into the dry ingredients and beat until smooth.

Spoon the mixture halfway up each case and bake for 25–30 minutes until risen and firm. Cool in the tins for 10 minutes, then turn out to cool on a wire rack.

To decorate the cupcakes, blend the icing sugar with 1 tablespoon warm water to make a thin glacé icing. Place in a paper icing bag and snip away the tip. Drizzle over the top of each cupcake in a lacy pattern. Keep in an airtight container for up to 5 days.

Try this: FOR AN ALTERNATIVE: 236 FOR A DINNER PARTY: 82

Mocha Cupcakes

MAKES 12

125 g/4 oz soft margarine
125 g/4 oz golden
  caster sugar
150 g/5 oz self-raising flour
2 tbsp cocoa powder
2 medium eggs

1 tbsp golden syrup
2 tbsp milk

To decorate:
225 g/8 oz golden
  icing sugar

125 g/4 oz unsalted
  butter, softened
2 tsp coffee extract
12 Cape gooseberries,
  papery covering
  pulled back

Preheat the oven to 180°C/350°F/Gas Mark 4, 10 minutes before baking. Line a 12-hole muffin tray with deep paper cases.

Place the margarine and sugar in a large bowl, then sift in the flour and cocoa powder. In another bowl, beat the eggs with the syrup, then add to the cocoa mixture. Whisk everything together with the milk using an electric beater for 2 minutes, or by hand with a wooden spoon.

Divide the mixture between the cases, filling them three-quarters full. Bake for about 20 minutes until the centres are springy to the touch. Turn out to cool on a wire rack.

Make the frosting by sifting the icing sugar into a bowl. Add the butter, coffee extract and 1 tablespoon hot water. Beat until fluffy, then swirl onto each cupcake with a flat-bladed knife. Top each with a fresh Cape gooseberry. Keep for 2 days in a cool place.

Try this: FOR AN ALTERNATIVE: 206   FOR A DINNER PARTY: 78

Crystallised Rosemary & Cranberry Cupcakes

MAKES 12

125 g/4 oz self-raising flour
125 g/4 oz butter, softened
125 g/4 oz golden
    caster sugar
2 medium eggs, beaten
zest of ½ orange,
    finely grated

To decorate:
1 egg white
12 small rosemary
    sprigs
125 g/4 oz fresh red
    cranberries
caster sugar, for dusting

3 tbsp apricot glaze, sieved
    (*see* page 26)
350 g/12 oz ready-to-roll
    sugarpaste
icing sugar, for dusting

Preheat the oven to 180°C/350°F/Gas Mark 4, 10 minutes before baking. Line a 12-hole bun tray with foil fairy-cake cases.

Sift the flour into a bowl and add the butter, sugar, eggs and orange zest. Beat for about 2 minutes until smooth, then spoon into the paper cases.

Bake in the centre of the preheated oven for about 14 minutes until well risen and springy in the centre. Transfer to a wire rack to cool.

To decorate, place a sheet of nonstick baking parchment on a flat surface. Beat the egg white until frothy, then brush thinly over the rosemary and cranberries and place them on the nonstick baking parchment. Dust with caster sugar and leave to dry out for 2–4 hours until crisp.

Brush the top of each fairy cake with a little apricot glaze. Roll out the sugarpaste on a clean, flat surface dusted with icing sugar and cut out 12 circles 6 cm/2½ inches wide. Place a disc on top of each and press level. Decorate each one with sparkly rosemary sprigs and cranberries. Keep for 3 days in an airtight container in a cool place.

Try this: FOR AN ALTERNATIVE: 218   FOR A DINNER PARTY: 66

Double Marble Cake

**CUTS INTO
8–10 SLICES**

75 g/3 oz white chocolate
75 g/3 oz dark chocolate
175 g/6 oz caster sugar
175 g/6 oz butter
4 medium eggs, separated
125 g/4 oz plain flour, sifted
75 g/3 oz ground almonds

For the topping:
125 ml/4 fl oz double cream
200 g/7 oz unsalted butter
100 g/3½ oz dark
   chocolate, chopped
100 g/3½ oz white
   chocolate, chopped

Preheat the oven to 180°C/350°F/Gas Mark 4, 10 minutes before baking. Lightly oil and line the base of a 20.5 cm/8 inch cake tin. Break the white and dark chocolate into small pieces, then place in two separate bowls placed over two pans of simmering water, ensuring that the bowls are not touching the water. Heat the chocolate until melted and smooth.

In a large bowl, cream the sugar and butter together until light and fluffy. Beat in the egg yolks one at a time and add a spoonful of flour after each addition. Stir in the ground almonds. In another bowl, whisk the egg whites until stiff. Gently fold the egg whites and the remaining sifted flour alternately into the almond mixture until all the flour and egg whites have been incorporated. Divide the mixture between two bowls. Gently stir the white chocolate into one bowl, then add the dark chocolate to the other bowl. Place alternating spoonfuls of the chocolate mixtures in the cake tin. Using a skewer, swirl the mixtures together to get a marbled effect, then tap the tin on the work surface to level the mixture. Bake in the oven for 40 minutes, or until cooked through, then leave to cool for 5 minutes in the tin before turning out onto a wire rack to cool completely.

For the topping, melt half of the cream and butter with the dark chocolate and the other half with the white chocolate and stir both until smooth. Cool, then whisk until thick and swirl both colours over the top of the cake to create a marbled effect.

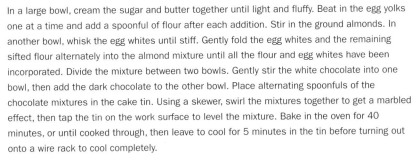

Try this: FOR AN ALTERNATIVE: 198   FOR A DINNER PARTY: 112

Sticky Toffee Cupcakes

MAKES 16–18

150 g/5 oz stoned
dates, chopped
1 tsp bicarbonate of soda
225 ml/8 fl oz hot water
175 g/6 oz plain flour
1 tsp baking powder

50 g/2 oz butter or block
margarine, diced
200 g/7 oz soft light
brown sugar
1 large egg, beaten
½ tsp vanilla extract

For the icing:
25 g/1 oz unsalted butter
5 tbsp soft light brown sugar
4 tbsp double cream

Preheat the oven to 180°C/350°F/Gas Mark 4, 10 minutes before baking. Line one or two bun trays with 16–18 fairy-cake cases, depending on the depth of the holes. Place the chopped dates in a bowl with the bicarbonate of soda and pour over the hot water. Stir, then set aside to cool.

Sift the flour and baking powder into a bowl and add the diced butter. Rub in between your fingertips until the mixture resembles fine crumbs. Stir in the sugar and mix well. Add the egg, vanilla extract and the date mixture. Beat with a wooden spoon until smooth.

Spoon into the cases and bake for about 25 minutes until well risen and firm to the touch in the centre. Leave to cool in the tins for 5 minutes, then turn out to cool on a wire rack.

To make the topping, place the butter, sugar and cream in a small pan over a low heat and stir until the sugar dissolves. Bring to the boil and boil for 1–2 minutes until the mixture thickens. Brush quickly over each fairy cake, as the mixture will set as it cools. Keep for 2 days in an airtight container.

Try this: FOR AN ALTERNATIVE: 236 FOR A DINNER PARTY: 38

Fresh Strawberry Sponge Cake

SERVES 8–10

175 g/6 oz unsalted
  butter, softened
175 g/6 oz caster sugar
1 tsp vanilla extract

3 large eggs, beaten
175 g/6 oz self-raising flour
150 ml/¼ pint double cream
2 tbsp icing sugar, sifted

225 g/8 oz fresh strawberries,
  hulled and chopped
few extra strawberries,
  to decorate

Preheat the oven to 190°C/375°F/Gas Mark 5, 10 minutes before baking. Lightly oil and line the bases of two 20.5 cm/8 inch round cake tins with greaseproof paper or baking parchment.

Using an electric whisk, beat the butter, sugar and vanilla extract together until pale and fluffy. Gradually beat in the eggs a little at a time, beating well after each addition.

Sift half the flour over the mixture and, using a metal spoon or rubber spatula, gently fold into the mixture. Sift over the remaining flour and fold in until just blended.

Divide the mixture between the tins, spreading evenly. Gently smooth the surfaces with the back of a spoon. Bake in the centre of the preheated oven for 20–25 minutes until well risen and golden.

Remove and leave to cool before turning out onto a wire rack. Whip the cream with 1 tablespoon of the icing sugar until it forms soft peaks. Fold in the chopped strawberries.

Spread one cake layer evenly with the mixture and top with the second cake layer, rounded-side up. Thickly dust the cake with icing sugar and decorate with the reserved strawberries. Carefully slide onto a serving plate and serve.

Try this: FOR AN ALTERNATIVE: 204 FOR A DINNER PARTY: 110

Shaggy Coconut Cupcakes

MAKES 12

½ tsp baking powder
200 g/7 oz self-raising flour
175 g/6 oz caster sugar
2 tbsp desiccated coconut
175 g/6 oz soft margarine
3 medium eggs, beaten
2 tbsp milk

To decorate:
1 batch buttercream
 (*see* page 24)
1 tbsp coconut liqueur
 (optional)
175 g/6 oz large shredded
 coconut strands

Preheat the oven to 180°C/350°F/Gas Mark 4, 10 minutes before baking. Line a 12-hole, deep muffin tray with paper cases.

Sift the baking powder and flour into a large bowl. Add all the remaining ingredients and beat for about 2 minutes until smooth and creamy. Divide evenly between the paper cases.

Bake in the preheated oven for 18–20 minutes until risen, golden and firm to the touch and a skewer inserted into the centre comes out clean. Leave in the muffin trays for 2 minutes, then turn out to cool on a wire rack.

To decorate the cupcakes, if you are using the coconut liqueur, beat this into the buttercream, and then swirl over each cupcake. To decorate, press large strands of shredded coconut into the buttercream. Keep for 3 days in an airtight container in a cool place.

Try this: FOR AN ALTERNATIVE: 202   FOR A DINNER PARTY: 58

Luxury Carrot Cake

CUTS INTO 12 SLICES

275 g/10 oz plain flour
2 tsp baking powder
1 tsp bicarbonate of soda
1 tsp salt
2 tsp ground cinnamon
1 tsp ground ginger
200 g/7 oz soft dark
    brown sugar
100 g/3½ oz caster sugar

4 large eggs, beaten
250 ml/8 fl oz sunflower oil
1 tbsp vanilla extract
4 carrots, peeled and
    shredded (about 450 g/1 lb)
400 g/14 oz can crushed
    pineapple, well drained
125 g/4 oz pecans or walnuts,
    toasted and chopped

For the frosting:
175 g/6 oz cream cheese,
    softened
50 g/2 oz butter, softened
1 tsp vanilla extract
225 g/8 oz icing sugar, sifted
1–2 tbsp milk, if needed

Preheat the oven to 180°C/350°F/Gas Mark 4, 10 minutes before baking. Lightly oil a 33 x 23 cm/ 13 x 9 inch baking tin. Line the base with nonstick baking parchment; oil and dust with flour.

Sift the first six ingredients into a large bowl and stir in the sugars to blend. Make a well in the centre.

Beat the eggs, oil and vanilla extract together and pour into the well. Using an electric whisk, gradually beat, drawing in the flour mixture from the sides until a smooth mixture forms. Stir in the carrots, crushed pineapple and chopped nuts until blended.

Pour into the prepared tin and smooth the surface evenly. Bake in the preheated oven for 50 minutes, or until firm and a skewer inserted into the centre comes out clean. Remove from the oven and leave to cool before removing from the tin and discarding the lining paper.

For the frosting, beat the cream cheese, butter and vanilla extract together until smooth, then gradually beat in the icing sugar until the frosting is smooth. Add a little milk, if necessary. Spread the frosting over the top. Refrigerate for about 1 hour to set the frosting, then cut into squares and serve.

Try this: FOR AN ALTERNATIVE: 246   FOR A DINNER PARTY: 76

Coffee & Walnut Fudge Cupcakes

MAKES 16–18

125 g/4 oz self-raising flour
125 g/4 oz butter, softened
125 g/4 oz golden
    caster sugar
2 medium eggs, beaten
1 tbsp golden syrup
50 g/2 oz walnuts,
    finely chopped

To decorate:
225 g/8 oz golden
    icing sugar
125 g/4 oz unsalted butter, at
    room temperature
2 tsp coffee extract
16–18 small walnut pieces

Preheat the oven to 200°C/400°F/Gas Mark 6, 10 minutes before baking. Line two 12-hole bun trays with 16–18 small foil cases, depending on the depth of the holes.

Stir the flour into a bowl and add the butter, sugar, eggs and syrup. Beat for about 2 minutes, then fold in the walnuts.

Spoon the mixture into the paper cases and bake for about 12–14 minutes until well risen and springy in the centre. Remove to a wire rack to cool.

Make the frosting by sifting the icing sugar into a bowl. Add the butter, coffee extract and 1 tablespoon hot water. Beat until light and fluffy, then place in a piping bag fitted with a star nozzle. Pipe a swirl on each cupcake and top with a walnut piece. Keep for 3–4 days in an airtight container in a cool place.

Try this: FOR AN ALTERNATIVE: 242 FOR A DINNER PARTY: 100

Lemony Coconut Cake

**CUTS INTO
10–12 SLICES**

275 g/10 oz plain flour
2 tbsp cornflour
1 tbsp baking powder
1 tsp salt
150 g/5 oz white vegetable
 fat or soft margarine
275 g/10 oz caster sugar
grated zest of 2 lemons

1 tsp vanilla extract
3 large eggs
150 ml/¼ pint milk
4 tbsp Malibu or rum
450 g/1 lb jar lemon curd
lime zest, to decorate

For the frosting:
275 g/10 oz caster sugar
125 ml/4 fl oz water
1 tbsp glucose
¼ tsp salt
1 tsp vanilla extract
3 large egg whites
75 g/3 oz desiccated coconut

Preheat the oven to 180°C/350°F/Gas Mark 4, 10 minutes before baking. Lightly oil and flour two 20.5 cm/8 inch, nonstick cake tins. Sift the flour, cornflour, baking powder and salt into a large bowl and add the white vegetable fat or margarine, sugar, lemon zest, vanilla extract, eggs and milk. With an electric whisk on a low speed, beat until blended, adding a little extra milk if the mixture is very stiff. Increase the speed to medium and beat for about 2 minutes.

Divide the mixture between the tins and smooth the surfaces evenly. Bake in the preheated oven for 20–25 minutes until the cakes feel firm and are cooked. Remove from the oven and cool before removing from the tins.

Put all the frosting ingredients except the coconut into a heatproof bowl placed over a saucepan of simmering water. Using an electric whisk, blend the frosting ingredients on a low speed. Increase the speed to high and beat for 7 minutes until the whites are stiff and glossy. Remove the bowl from the heat and continue beating until cool. Cover with clingfilm.

Using a serrated knife, split the cake layers horizontally in half and sprinkle each cut surface with the Malibu or rum. Sandwich the cakes together with the lemon curd and press lightly. Spread the top and sides generously with the frosting, swirling and peaking the top. Sprinkle the coconut over the top of the cake and gently press onto the sides to cover. Decorate with the lime zest. Serve.

Try this: FOR AN ALTERNATIVE: 232   FOR A DINNER PARTY: 92

Lamington Cupcakes

MAKES 12

125 g/4 oz self-raising flour
125 g/4 oz butter, softened
125 g/4 oz golden
   caster sugar
2 medium eggs, beaten

1 tsp vanilla extract

To decorate:
350 g/12 oz caster sugar
1 tbsp cocoa powder

125 ml/4 fl oz water
65 g/2½ oz desiccated
   coconut
ready-made chocolate
   decorations

Preheat the oven to 180°C/350°F/Gas Mark 4, 10 minutes before baking. Line a 12-hole muffin tray with deep paper cases.

Sift the flour into a bowl and add the butter, sugar, eggs and vanilla extract. Beat for about two minutes until smooth, then spoon into the paper cases.

Bake in the centre of the preheated oven for about 18 minutes until well risen and springy in the centre. Transfer to a wire rack to cool.

To make the icing, place the caster sugar, cocoa powder and water in a large, heavy-based pan. Heat over a low heat until every grain of sugar has dissolved. Bring to the boil and then simmer for about 6 minutes, without stirring, until thickened into a syrup. Pour into a bowl and use the syrup while it is still hot, as it will set as it cools.

Place the coconut into a large bowl. Dip the top of each cupcake into the hot chocolate syrup to coat the top, then dip in coconut, decorate and place on a tray to dry. Keep for 2–3 days in an airtight container.

Try this: FOR AN ALTERNATIVE: 254   FOR A DINNER PARTY: 74

Wild Strawberry & Rose Petal Jam Cake

SERVES 8

275 g/10 oz plain flour
1 tsp baking powder
¼ tsp salt
150 g/5 oz unsalted butter,
    softened
200 g/7 oz caster sugar
2 large eggs, beaten
2 tbsp rosewater
125 ml/4 fl oz milk

125 g/4 oz rose petal
    or strawberry jam,
    slightly warmed
125 g/4 oz wild strawberries,
    hulled, or baby
    strawberries, chopped
frosted rose petals,
    to decorate

For the rose cream filling:
200 ml/7 fl oz double cream
25 ml/1 fl oz natural
    Greek yogurt
2 tbsp rosewater
1 tbsp icing sugar, plus extra
    for dusting

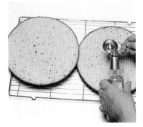

Preheat the oven to 180°C/350°F/Gas Mark 4, 10 minutes before baking. Lightly oil and flour a 20.5 cm/8 inch, nonstick cake tin. Sift the flour, baking powder and salt into a bowl and reserve.

Beat the butter and sugar together until light and fluffy. Beat in the eggs a little at a time, then stir in the rosewater. Gently fold in the flour mixture and milk with a metal spoon or rubber spatula and mix lightly together. Spoon the cake mixture into the tin, spreading evenly and smoothing the surface.

Bake in the preheated oven for 25–30 minutes until well risen and golden and the centre springs back when pressed with a clean finger. Remove and cool, then remove from the tin.

For the filling, whisk the cream, yogurt, 1 tablespoon of the rosewater and 1 tablespoon icing sugar until soft peaks form. Split the cake horizontally in half and sprinkle with the remaining rosewater.

Spread the warmed jam onto one of the cake layers. Top with half the whipped cream mixture, then sprinkle with half the strawberries. Place the remaining cake half on top. Spread with the remaining cream and swirl, if desired. Decorate with the rose petals. Dust the cake lightly with a little icing sugar and serve.

Try this: FOR AN ALTERNATIVE: 240   FOR A DINNER PARTY: 48

Kids' Parties

Pink Party Piggies

MAKES 12

125 g/4 oz caster sugar
125 g/4 oz soft tub
 margarine
2 medium eggs
1 tbsp milk
125 g/4 oz self-raising flour
½ tsp baking powder

To decorate:
1 batch buttercream
 (*see* page 24)
pink liquid food colouring
pink marshmallows
edible gold or silver balls

Preheat the oven to 190°C/375°F/Gas Mark 5, 10 minutes before baking. Line a bun tray with 12 small paper cases.

Place all the cupcake ingredients in a large bowl and beat with an electric mixer for about 2 minutes until smooth. Half-fill the paper cases with the mixture.

Bake for about 15 minutes until firm, risen and golden. Set on a wire rack to cool.

To decorate, mix the buttercream with the pink food colouring until it is pale pink. Spread smoothly over the top of each cupcake with a small palette knife. Cut a slice from a pink marshmallow with wetted scissors, then cut this in half to form the ears and press into the buttercream. Place a large halved marshmallow in the centre to form the snout. Add edible gold or silver balls to form eyes. Keep for 2–3 days sealed in an airtight container.

Try this: FOR AN ALTERNATIVE: 296 FOR A TEA PARTY: 212

Birthday Numbers Cupcakes

MAKES 12–14

125 g/4 oz self-raising flour
125 g/4 oz caster sugar
125 g/4 oz soft margarine
2 medium eggs, beaten
1 tsp vanilla extract

To decorate:
225 g/8 oz ready-to-roll
   sugarpaste
paste food colourings

icing sugar, for dusting
1 batch buttercream
   (*see* page 24)
small candles
sprinkles and decorations

Preheat the oven to 180°C/350°F/Gas Mark 4, 10 minutes before baking. Line one or two 12-hole bun trays with 12–14 paper fairy-cake cases or silicone moulds, depending on the depth of the holes.

Sift the flour into a bowl and stir together with the caster sugar. Add the margarine, eggs and vanilla extract and beat together for about 2 minutes until smooth.

Spoon into the cases and bake in the preheated oven for 15–20 minutes until golden and firm to the touch. Turn out onto a wire rack. When cool, trim the tops flat if they have peaked slightly.

To decorate, colour batches of sugarpaste in bright colours. Dust a clean surface lightly with icing sugar. Thinly roll each colour of sugarpaste and cut out numbers using a set of cutters. Leave these for 2 hours to dry and harden.

Using a palette knife, spread the buttercream thickly onto the top of each cupcake. Place a small candle into each cupcake and stand the number up against this. Coat the edges of each cupcake with sprinkles and decorations. Serve within 8 hours as the numbers may start to soften.

Try this: FOR AN ALTERNATIVE: 288   FOR A TEA PARTY: 230

Pirate Cupcakes

MAKES 14–16

125 g/4 oz self-raising flour
125 g/4 oz caster sugar
125 g/4 oz soft margarine
2 medium eggs, beaten
1 tsp vanilla extract

To decorate:
125 g/4 oz buttercream
  (*see* page 24)
450 g/1 lb ready-to-roll
  sugarpaste

pink, yellow, blue and black
  paste food colourings
small sweets and edible
  coloured balls
small tube red gel icing

Preheat the oven to 180°C/350°F/Gas Mark 4. Line two 12-hole bun trays with 14–16 paper fairy-cake cases or silicone moulds, depending on the depth of the holes.

Sift the flour into a bowl and stir together with the caster sugar. Add the margarine, eggs and vanilla extract and beat together for about 2 minutes until smooth.

Divide the mixture between the cases and bake in the preheated oven for 15–20 minutes until golden and firm to the touch. Turn out onto a wire rack. When cool, trim the tops flat if they have peaked slightly.

To decorate, lightly coat the top of each cupcake with a little buttercream. Colour the sugarpaste pale pink and roll out thinly on a surface dusted with icing sugar. Stamp out circles 6 cm/2½ inches wide and place these on the buttercream to cover the top of each cupcake.

Colour some scraps of sugarpaste blue, some yellow and a small amount black. Make triangular shapes from the blue and yellow icing and place these onto the pink icing at an angle to form hats. Stick coloured edible balls into the icing to decorate the hats. Make thin sausages from the black icing and press these across the cupcakes, then make tiny eye patches from black icing. Stick on a tiny sweet for each eye and pipe on red mouths with the gel icing. Keep for 2 days in an airtight container.

Try this: FOR AN ALTERNATIVE: 296 FOR A TEA PARTY: 234

All-in-one Chocolate Fudge Cakes

MAKES 15

175 g/6 oz soft dark
   brown sugar
175 g/6 oz butter, softened
150 g/5 oz self-raising flour
25 g/1 oz cocoa powder
½ tsp baking powder
pinch salt

3 medium eggs, lightly beaten
1 tbsp golden syrup

For the fudge topping:
75 g/3 oz granulated sugar
150 ml/¼ pint evaporated milk

175 g/6 oz dark chocolate,
   roughly chopped
40 g/1½ oz unsalted butter,
   softened
125 g/4 oz soft fudge sweets,
   finely chopped

Preheat the oven to 180°C/350°F/Gas Mark 4, 10 minutes before baking. Oil and line a
28 x 18 x 2.5 cm/11 x 7 x 1 inch cake tin with nonstick baking parchment.

Place the soft brown sugar and butter in a bowl and sift in the flour, cocoa powder, baking
powder and salt. Add the eggs and golden syrup, then beat with an electric whisk for 2
minutes before adding 2 tablespoons warm water and beating for a further 1 minute.

Turn the mixture into the prepared tin and level the top with the back of a spoon. Bake on the
centre shelf of the preheated oven for 30 minutes, or until firm to the touch. Turn the cake out
onto a wire rack and leave to cool before removing the baking parchment.

To make the topping, gently heat the sugar and evaporated milk in a saucepan, stirring
frequently, until the sugar has dissolved. Bring the mixture to the boil and simmer for 6
minutes without stirring.

Remove the mixture from the heat. Add the chocolate and butter and stir until melted and
blended. Pour into a bowl and chill in the refrigerator for 1–2 hours until thickened. Spread the
topping over the cake, then sprinkle with the chopped fudge. Cut the cake into 15 squares
before serving.

Try this: FOR AN ALTERNATIVE: 306 FOR A TEA PARTY: 190

Butterfly Wings & Flowers Cupcakes

MAKES 12–14

150 g/5 oz butter, softened
150 g/5 oz caster sugar
175 g/5 oz self-raising flour
3 medium eggs, beaten
1 tsp lemon juice
2 tbsp milk

To decorate:
350 g/12 oz ready-to-roll
   sugarpaste
paste food colourings
icing sugar, for dusting
1 batch cream cheese
   frosting (*see* page 24)
gel icing tubes

Preheat the oven to 180°C/350°F/Gas Mark 4, 10 minutes before baking. Line one or two 12-hole muffin trays with 12–14 deep paper cases, depending on the depth of the holes.

Place the butter and sugar in a bowl, then sift in the flour. Add the beaten eggs to the bowl with the lemon juice and milk and beat until smooth. Spoon into the cases, filling them three-quarters full.

Bake in the preheated oven for about 18 minutes until firm to the touch in the centre. Turn out to cool on a wire rack.

To decorate, colour the sugarpaste in batches of lilac, blue, pink and yellow. Dust a clean, flat surface with icing sugar. Roll out the sugarpaste thinly and mark out daisy shapes (*see also* page 126) and butterfly wings. Leave these to dry for 30 minutes until firm enough to handle.

Place the frosting in a piping bag fitted with a star nozzle and pipe swirls onto each cupcake. Press the wings and flowers onto the frosting and pipe on decorations with small gel icing tubes. Keep in an airtight container in a cool place for 3 days.

Try this: FOR AN ALTERNATIVE: 312   FOR A TEA PARTY: 238

Football Cupcakes

MAKES 12–14

125 g/4 oz self-raising flour
125 g/4 oz caster sugar
125 g/4 oz soft margarine
2 medium eggs, beaten
1 tsp vanilla extract

To decorate:
125 g/4 oz buttercream
 (*see* page 24)
600 g/1 lb 5 oz ready-to-roll
 sugarpaste

icing sugar, for dusting
black paste food colouring

Preheat the oven to 180°C/350°F/Gas Mark 4, 10 minutes before baking. Line two 12-hole bun trays with 12–14 paper fairy-cake cases or silicone moulds, depending on the depth of the holes.

Sift the flour into a bowl and stir together with the caster sugar. Add the margarine, eggs and vanilla extract and beat together for about 2 minutes until smooth.

Spoon into the cases and bake in the preheated oven for 15–20 minutes until golden and firm to the touch. Turn out onto a wire rack. When cool, trim the tops flat if they have peaked slightly.

To decorate, lightly coat the top of each cupcake with a little buttercream. Roll out the white sugarpaste on a surface dusted with icing sugar and cut out circles 6 cm/2½ inches wide and place these on the buttercream to cover the top of each cupcake. Colour 75 g/3 oz of the scraps black.

Using a small icing nozzle as a round guide, stamp out small white and black discs. Cut six straight edges away from the circles to form hexagons. Dampen the back of each hexagon with a little water, then stick the black discs between white ones, carefully matching up all the edges so they fit together. Keep for 3 days in an airtight container.

Chocolate Fudge Brownies

MAKES 16

125 g/4 oz butter
175 g/6 oz plain dark
   chocolate, roughly
   chopped or broken
225 g/8 oz caster sugar
2 tsp vanilla extract

2 medium eggs,
   lightly beaten
150 g/5 oz plain flour

For the icing:
175 g/6 oz icing sugar
2 tbsp cocoa powder
15 g/½ oz butter

Preheat the oven to 180°C/350°F/Gas Mark 4, 10 minutes before baking. Lightly oil and line a 20.5 cm/8 inch, square cake tin with greaseproof paper or baking parchment.

Slowly melt the butter and chocolate together in a heatproof bowl set over a saucepan of simmering water. Transfer the mixture to a large bowl.

Stir in the sugar and vanilla extract, then stir in the eggs. Sift over the flour and fold together well with a metal spoon or rubber spatula. Pour into the prepared tin.

Transfer to the preheated oven and bake for 30 minutes until just set. Remove the cooked mixture from the oven and leave to cool in the tin before turning it out onto a wire rack.

For the icing, sift the icing sugar and cocoa powder into a small bowl and make a well in the centre. Place the butter in the well, then gradually add about 2 tablespoons hot water. Mix to form a smooth, spreadable icing.

Pour the icing over the cooked mixture. Allow the icing to set before cutting into squares. Serve the brownies when they are cold.

Try this: FOR AN ALTERNATIVE: 280   FOR A TEA PARTY: 198

Boys' & Girls' Names

MAKES 16–18

175 g/6 oz self-raising flour
175 g/6 oz caster sugar
175 g/6 oz soft margarine
3 medium eggs, beaten
1 tsp vanilla extract

To decorate:
1 batch buttercream
  (*see* page 24)
paste food colourings
sprinkles and decorations
gel writing icing tubes

Preheat the oven to 180°C/350°F/Gas Mark 4, 10 minutes before baking. Line two 12-hole bun trays with 16–18 paper fairy-cake cases or silicone moulds, depending on the depth of the holes.

Sift the flour into a bowl and stir together with the caster sugar. Add the margarine, eggs and vanilla extract and beat together for about 2 minutes until smooth.

Spoon into the cases and bake in the preheated oven for 15–20 minutes until golden and firm to the touch. Turn out onto a wire rack. When cool, trim the tops flat if they have peaked slightly.

Divide the buttercream into batches and colour pink, green and yellow. Spread the icing over the cakes. Coat the edges of each fairy cake with brightly coloured sprinkles, then add a name in the centre of each one with the writing icing. Keep in an airtight container in a cool place for 2 days.

Try this: FOR AN ALTERNATIVE: 300   FOR A TEA PARTY: 230

Jellybean Cupcakes

MAKES 12–14

125 g/4 oz self-raising flour
125 g/4 oz caster sugar
125 g/4 oz soft margarine
2 medium eggs, beaten
1 tsp vanilla extract

To decorate:
1 batch buttercream
    (*see* page 24)
colourful jellybeans or
    candied jelly shapes

Preheat the oven to 180°C/350°F/Gas Mark 4, 10 minutes before baking. Line two 12-hole bun trays with 12–14 paper fairy-cake cases or silicone moulds, depending on the depth of the holes.

Sift the flour into a bowl and stir together with the caster sugar. Add the margarine, eggs and vanilla extract and beat together for about 2 minutes until smooth.

Spoon into the cases and bake in the preheated oven for 15–20 minutes until golden and firm to the touch. Turn out to cool on a wire rack.

When completely cold, swirl buttercream icing all over the tops of the cupcakes and decorate by pressing on coloured jellybeans. Keep for 3 days in an airtight container in a cool place.

Try this: FOR AN ALTERNATIVE: 308 FOR A TEA PARTY: 228

Teddy Bear Cupcakes

MAKES 14–16

125 g/4 oz self-raising flour
125 g/4 oz caster sugar
125 g/4 oz soft margarine
2 medium eggs, beaten
1 tsp vanilla extract

To decorate:
225 g/8 oz ready-to-roll
   sugarpaste
brown paste food
   colouring

325 g/11½ oz fondant
   icing sugar, plus extra
   for dusting
6 tbsp royal icing sugar

Preheat the oven to 180°C/350°F/Gas Mark 4, 10 minutes before baking. Line two 12-hole bun trays with 14–16 paper fairy-cake cases or silicone moulds, depending on the depth of the holes.

Sift the flour into a bowl and stir together with the caster sugar. Add the margarine, eggs and vanilla extract and beat together for about 2 minutes until smooth.

Spoon into the cases and bake in the preheated oven for 15–20 minutes until golden and firm to the touch. Turn out on a wire rack. When cool, trim the tops flat if they have peaked slightly.

Colour the sugarpaste icing golden brown. Dust a small board with icing sugar. Roll the coloured sugarpaste thinly and stamp out bear shapes with a small cutter or trace round a pattern and mark onto the sugarpaste with a sharp knife. Leave to dry for 30 minutes.

Mix the fondant icing sugar with enough cold water to form a stiff, shiny icing of coating consistency and colour this light brown. Flood the icing on top of each cupcake and, while still wet, place the bear shape onto this.

Mix the royal icing sugar with a little water to make a stiff paste and then pipe on eyes, a nose and buttons. Leave to set for 30 minutes. Keep for 1 day in an airtight container.

Try this: FOR AN ALTERNATIVE: 274   FOR A TEA PARTY: 234

Glittery Outer Space Cupcakes

MAKES 18–20

125 g/4 oz soft margarine
125 g/4 oz caster sugar
125 g/4 oz self-raising flour
2 medium eggs
1 tsp vanilla extract
1 tbsp milk

To decorate:
125 g/4 oz ready-to-roll
  sugarpaste
edible coloured or
  glitter dust
1 batch cream cheese
  frosting (*see* page 24)

edible metallic
  coloured balls

Preheat the oven to 180°C/350°F/Gas Mark 4, 10 minutes before baking. Line a mini-muffin tray with 18–20 mini paper cases or silicone moulds, depending on the depth of the holes.

Place the margarine and sugar in a bowl, then sift in the flour. In another bowl, beat the eggs with the vanilla extract and milk, then add to the flour mixture. Beat until smooth, then spoon into the cases, filling them halfway up.

Bake in the preheated oven for about 12–14 minutes until firm to the touch in the centre. Turn out to cool on a wire rack.

Place a large piece of nonstick baking parchment on a flat surface. Roll the sugarpaste into pea-size balls on the paper. Coat the balls with edible coloured or glitter dust. Leave to dry out for 2 hours until firm. Place the frosting in a piping bag fitted with a star nozzle and pipe swirls on top of each cupcake. Top each cupcake with the coloured sugarpaste balls and edible metallic balls. Keep for 2 days in an airtight container in a cool place.

Try this: FOR AN ALTERNATIVE: 304 FOR A TEA PARTY: 188

Kitty Faces Cupcakes

MAKES 14–16

125 g/4 oz self-raising flour
125 g/4 oz caster sugar
125 g/4 oz soft margarine
2 medium eggs, beaten
1 tsp vanilla extract

To decorate:
1 batch buttercream
  (*see* page 24)
pink paste food colouring
50 g/2 oz desiccated coconut

Liquorice Allsorts sweets
red gel writing icing tube

Preheat the oven to 180°C/350°F/Gas Mark 4, 10 minutes before baking. Line two 12-hole bun trays with 14–16 paper fairy-cake cases or silicone moulds, depending on the depth of the holes.

Sift the flour into a bowl and stir together with the caster sugar. Add the margarine, eggs and vanilla extract and beat together for about 2 minutes until smooth.

Spoon into the cases and bake in the preheated oven for 15–20 minutes until golden and firm to the touch. Turn out onto a wire rack. When cool, trim the tops flat if they have peaked slightly.

Colour the buttercream pink and spread over the top of each cupcake. Pour the coconut onto a shallow dish. Press the top of each iced cupcake into the coconut.

Cut the sweets to form pink ears, eyes, a jelly nose and whiskers and pipe on a red mouth in red gel icing. Keep in an airtight container in a cool place for 2 days.

Try this: FOR AN ALTERNATIVE: 292   FOR A TEA PARTY: 222

Fast Cars Cupcakes

MAKE 12–14

125 g/4 oz self-raising flour
1 tbsp cocoa powder
125 g/4 oz caster sugar
125 g/4 oz soft margarine
2 medium eggs, beaten
1 tsp vanilla extract

To decorate:
225 g/8 oz ready-to-roll
    sugarpaste
red and blue paste food
    colourings
icing sugar, for dusting

350 g/12 oz fondant icing
    sugar, sifted
6 tbsp royal icing sugar

Preheat the oven to 180°C/350°F/Gas Mark 4, 10 minutes before baking. Line two 12-hole bun trays with 12–14 paper fairy-cake cases or silicone moulds, depending on the depth of the holes.

Sift the flour and cocoa powder into a bowl and stir together with the caster sugar. Add the margarine, eggs and vanilla extract and beat together for about 2 minutes until smooth.

Spoon into the cases and bake in the preheated oven for 15–20 minutes until golden and firm to the touch. Turn out on a wire rack. When cool, trim the tops flat if they have peaked slightly.

To decorate, colour half the sugarpaste blue and half red. Dust a clean surface lightly with icing sugar. Roll each colour out thinly and cut out little car shapes. Leave these for 2 hours to dry and harden.

Blend the fondant icing sugar with enough water to make an icing to a coating consistency. Spread over the top of each cupcake and, while still wet, place a car shape in the centre of each one. Mix the royal icing sugar with enough water to make a piping icing. Place this in a small paper icing bag with the end snipped away. Pipe wheels and windows on the cars and leave the cupcakes to dry for 30 minutes. Keep for 3 days in an airtight container.

Try this: FOR AN ALTERNATIVE: 284   FOR A TEA PARTY: 192

Colourful Letters Cupcakes

MAKES 12–14

125 g/4 oz self-raising flour
125 g/4 oz caster sugar
125 g/4 oz soft margarine
2 medium eggs, beaten
1 tsp vanilla extract

To decorate:
225 g/8 oz ready-to-roll
  sugarpaste
paste food colourings

350 g/12 oz icing sugar,
  sifted, plus extra
  for dusting
small coloured sweets

Preheat the oven to 180°C/350°F/Gas Mark 4, 10 minutes before baking. Line two 12-hole bun trays with 12–14 paper fairy-cake cases or silicone moulds, depending on the depth of the holes.

Sift the flour into a bowl and stir together with the caster sugar. Add the margarine, eggs and vanilla extract and beat together for about 2 minutes until smooth.

Spoon into the cases and bake in the preheated oven for 15–20 minutes until golden and firm to the touch. Turn out onto a wire rack. When cool, trim the tops flat if they have peaked slightly.

To decorate, colour batches of sugarpaste in bright colours. Dust a clean surface lightly with icing sugar. Roll each colour out thinly and cut out letters using a set of cutters or tracing round patterns.

Blend the icing sugar with 1 teaspoon water to make a glacé icing of coating consistency. Spread over the top of each cupcake and place a bright letter in the centre of each one. Decorate round the edges with coloured sweets and leave the cupcakes to dry for 30 minutes. Keep for 3 days in an airtight container.

Try this: FOR AN ALTERNATIVE: 276 FOR A TEA PARTY: 230

Goth Cupcakes

MAKES 12–14

125 g/4 oz self-raising flour
125 g/4 oz caster sugar
125 g/4 oz soft margarine
2 medium eggs, beaten
1 tsp vanilla extract

To decorate:
350 g/12 oz fondant icing
　sugar, sifted
black and green paste
　food colourings

edible silver balls and
　decorations

Preheat the oven to 180°C/350°F/Gas Mark 4, 10 minutes before baking. Line two 12-hole bun trays with 12–14 paper fairy-cake cases or silicone moulds, depending on the depth of the holes.

Sift the flour into a bowl and stir together with the caster sugar. Add the margarine, eggs and vanilla extract and beat together for about 2 minutes until smooth.

Spoon into the cases and bake in the preheated oven for 15–20 minutes until golden and firm to the touch. Turn out onto a wire rack. When cool, trim the tops flat if they have peaked slightly.

To decorate, blend the fondant icing sugar with enough water to make a coating consistency. Colour half the icing black and half green. Spread over the top of each cupcake and place the silver balls round the outer edges. Decorate with metallic cake shapes and dry for 30 minutes. Keep for 2 days in an airtight container in a cool place.

Try this: FOR AN ALTERNATIVE: 308   FOR A TEA PARTY: 234

Starry Cupcakes

MAKES 12

125 g/4 oz butter, softened
125 g/4 oz caster sugar
125 g/4 oz self-raising flour
2 medium eggs
1 tsp vanilla extract

To decorate:
icing sugar, for dusting
225 g/8 oz ready-to-roll
   sugarpaste
dust or paste food
   colourings

1 batch cream cheese
   frosting (*see* page 24)
edible silver ball decorations
   (optional)
small candles

Preheat the oven to 180˚C/350˚F/Gas Mark 4, 10 minutes before baking. Line a 12-hole muffin tray with deep paper cases.

Place the butter and sugar in a bowl, then sift in the flour. In another bowl, beat the eggs with the vanilla extract, then add to the flour mixture. Beat until smooth, then spoon into the cases, filling them three-quarters full.

Bake in the preheated oven for about 18 minutes until firm to the touch in the centre. Turn out to cool on a wire rack.

To decorate the cupcakes, dust a clean, flat surface with icing sugar. Colour the sugarpaste in batches of bright colours, such as blue, yellow and orange. Roll each out thinly and cut out stars with a cutter. Leave to dry out for 2 hours until firm.

Place the frosting in a piping bag fitted with a star nozzle and pipe large swirls on top of each cupcake. Decorate each cupcake with stars, edible silver balls, if using, and small candles. Keep for 2 days in an airtight container in a cool place.

Try this: FOR AN ALTERNATIVE: 294   FOR A TEA PARTY: 208

**MAKES 12 LARGE
CUPCAKES OR
18 FAIRY CAKES**

Chocolate Fudge Flake Cupcakes

125 g/4 oz self-raising flour
25 g/1 oz cocoa powder
125 g/4 oz soft margarine
125 g/4 oz soft light
   brown sugar
2 medium eggs, beaten
2 tbsp milk

To decorate:
25 g/1 oz butter
50 g/2 oz golden syrup
15 g/^{1}/$_2$ oz cocoa powder
125 g/4 oz golden
   icing sugar
25 g/1 oz cream cheese

40 g/1½ oz chocolate
   flake bars

Preheat the oven to 180°C/350°F/Gas Mark 4, 10 minutes before baking. Line a 12-hole muffin tray with deep paper cases, or one or two bun trays with 18 fairy-cake cases.

Sift the flour and cocoa powder into a large bowl, add the margarine, sugar, eggs and milk and whisk with an electric beater for about 2 minutes until smooth.

Divide the mixture between the paper cases and bake in the preheated oven for about 20 minutes for the larger cupcakes and 15 minutes for the fairy cakes until a skewer inserted into the centre comes out clean. Turn out to cool on a wire rack.

To make the topping, melt the butter with the syrup and cocoa powder in a pan. Cool, then whisk in the icing sugar until the mixture has thickened, and beat in the cream cheese. Spread the frosting over the cupcakes. Chop the flake bars into small chunks, then place one chunk in the centre of each cupcake. Keep for 2–3 days in the refrigerator.

Try this: FOR AN ALTERNATIVE: 310   FOR A TEA PARTY: 240

Polka Dot Cupcakes

MAKES 12

150 g/5 oz butter, softened
150 g/5 oz caster sugar
175 g/6 oz self-raising flour
3 medium eggs
1 tsp vanilla extract
2 tbsp milk

To decorate:
1 batch cream cheese
    frosting (*see* page 24)
125 g/4 oz ready-to-roll
    sugarpaste
paste food colourings
icing sugar, for dusting

Preheat the oven to 180°C/350°F/Gas Mark 4, 10 minutes before baking. Line a 12-hole muffin tray with paper cases.

Place the butter and sugar in a bowl, then sift in the flour. In another bowl, beat the eggs with the vanilla extract and milk, then add to the flour mixture and beat until smooth. Spoon into the cases, filling them three-quarters full.

Bake in the preheated oven for about 18 minutes until firm to the touch in the centre. Turn out to cool on a wire rack.

To decorate, swirl the top of each cupcake with a little cream cheese frosting using a small palette knife. Divide the sugarpaste into batches and colour each one separately with paste food colouring. Dust a clean, flat surface with icing sugar. Roll out the coloured icing and stamp out small coloured circles with the flat end of an icing nozzle. Press the dots onto the frosting. Keep for 3 days in an airtight container in a cool place.

Try this: FOR AN ALTERNATIVE: 302   FOR A TEA PARTY: 230

Rocky Road Cupcakes

MAKES 14–18

125 g/4 oz self-raising flour
25 g/1 oz cocoa powder
125 g/4 oz soft dark
  brown sugar
125 g/4 oz soft margarine
2 medium eggs, beaten
2 tbsp milk

To decorate:
75 g/3 oz dark chocolate,
  broken into squares
40 g/1½ oz butter
75 g/3 oz mini
  marshmallows
40 g/1½ oz chopped
  mixed nuts

Preheat the oven to 180°C/350°F/Gas Mark 4, 10 minutes before baking. Line one or two bun trays with 14–18 paper cases or silicone moulds, depending on the depth of the holes.

Sift the flour and cocoa powder into a large bowl. Add the sugar, margarine, eggs and milk and whisk with an electric beater for about 2 minutes until smooth. Divide the mixture evenly between the paper cases and bake in the preheated oven for about 20 minutes until a skewer inserted into the centre comes out clean. Remove the trays from the oven but leave the oven on.

For the topping, gently melt the chocolate and butter together in a small pan over a low heat. Place the melted chocolate mixture in an icing bag made of greaseproof paper and snip away the end. Pipe a little of the mixture on top of each cupcake, then scatter the marshmallows and nuts over each one and return to the oven. Bake for 2–3 minutes to soften the marshmallows.

Remove from the oven and pipe the remaining chocolate over the marshmallows. Leave to cool in the trays for 5 minutes, then remove to cool on a wire rack. Serve warm or cold. Keep for 2 days in an airtight container.

Try this: FOR AN ALTERNATIVE: 286   FOR A TEA PARTY: 264

Pink Butterfly Cakes

MAKES 12

150 g/5 oz butter, softened, at room temperature
150 g/5 oz caster sugar
3 medium eggs, beaten
1 tsp vanilla extract

150 g /5 oz self-raising flour
½ tsp baking powder

To decorate:
pink and brown paste food colourings

225 g/8 oz ready-to-roll sugarpaste
1 batch cream cheese frosting (*see* page 24)
gel writing icing tubes

Preheat the oven to 180°C/350°F/Gas Mark 4, 10 minutes before baking and line a 12-hole muffin tray with deep paper cases.

Place the butter, sugar, eggs and vanilla extract in a bowl and then sift in the flour and baking powder. Beat together for about 2 minutes with an electric hand mixer until pale and fluffy. Spoon into the paper cases and bake in the preheated oven for 20–25 minutes until firm and golden. Cool on a wire rack.

To decorate the cupcakes, colour 200 g/7 oz of the sugarpaste pale pink and colour the remainder brown. Roll out the sugarpaste thinly and, using a cutter, cut out four petal shapes for the wings for each cupcake and set them on nonstick baking parchment or clingfilm. Cut out 48 shapes altogether and leave to dry flat until firm (about 2 hours). Colour the cream cheese frosting bright pink and place in a piping bag fitted with a star nozzle.

Pipe a swirl of pink frosting to cover the top of each cupcake and then press four wings on top of each. Mould the brown icing into a thin body shape and place on each cupcake. Pipe dots on the wings with tubes of gel writing icing. Keep for 2 days in an airtight container in a cool place.

Try this: FOR AN ALTERNATIVE: 274 FOR A TEA PARTY: 222

Outdoor Parties

Fruit & Spice Chocolate Slice

CUTS INTO 10 SLICES

350 g/12 oz self-raising flour
1 tsp ground mixed spice
175 g/6 oz butter, chilled
125 g/4 oz dark chocolate,
   roughly chopped

125 g/4 oz dried mixed fruit
75 g/3 oz dried apricots,
   chopped
75 g/3 oz chopped
   mixed nuts

175 g/6 oz demerara sugar
2 medium eggs, lightly
   beaten
150 ml/¼ pint milk

Preheat the oven to 180°C/350°F/Gas Mark 4, 10 minutes before baking. Oil and line a deep, 18 cm/7 inch, square tin with nonstick baking parchment. Sift the flour and mixed spice into a large bowl. Cut the butter into small squares and, using your hands, rub in until the mixture resembles fine breadcrumbs.

Add the chocolate, dried mixed fruit, apricots and nuts to the dry ingredients. Reserve 1 tablespoon of the sugar, then add the rest to the bowl and stir together. Add the eggs and half of the milk and mix together, then add enough of the remaining milk to give a soft dropping consistency.

Spoon the mixture into the prepared tin, level the surface with the back of a spoon and sprinkle with the reserved demerara sugar. Bake on the centre shelf of the preheated oven for 50 minutes. Cover the top with foil to prevent the cake from browning too much and bake for a further 30–40 minutes until it is firm to the touch and a skewer inserted into the centre of the cake comes out clean.

Leave the cake in the tin for 10 minutes to cool slightly, then turn out onto a wire rack and leave to cool completely. Cut into 10 slices and serve. Store in an airtight container.

Try this: FOR AN ALTERNATIVE: 322   FOR A DINNER PARTY: 68

Chunky Chocolate Muffins

MAKES 7

50 g/2 oz dark chocolate,
   roughly chopped
50 g/2 oz light muscovado
   sugar
25 g/1 oz butter, melted
125 ml/4 fl oz milk, heated to
   room temperature
½ tsp vanilla extract

1 medium egg,
   lightly beaten
150 g/5 oz self-raising flour
½ tsp baking powder
pinch salt
75 g/3 oz white chocolate,
   chopped
2 tsp icing sugar (optional)

Preheat the oven to 200°C/400°F/Gas Mark 6, 15 minutes before baking. Line a muffin or deep bun tray with seven paper muffin cases or oil the individual compartments well. Place the plain chocolate in a large, heatproof bowl set over a saucepan of simmering water and stir occasionally until melted. Remove the bowl and leave to cool for a few minutes.

Stir the sugar and butter into the melted chocolate, then the milk, vanilla extract and egg. Sift in the flour, baking powder and salt together. Add the chopped white chocolate, then, using a metal spoon, fold together quickly, taking care not to overmix.

Divide the mixture between the paper cases, piling it up in the centre. Bake on the centre shelf of the preheated oven for 20–25 minutes until well risen and firm to the touch.

Lightly dust the tops of the muffins with icing sugar, if using, as soon as they come out of the oven. Leave the muffins in the tray for a few minutes, then transfer to a wire rack. Serve warm or cold.

Try this: FOR AN ALTERNATIVE: 344 FOR A DINNER PARTY: 84

Jammy Buns

MAKES 12

175 g/6 oz plain flour
175 g/6 oz wholemeal flour
2 tsp baking powder
150 g/5 oz butter or
   margarine
125 g/4 oz golden
   caster sugar

50 g/2 oz dried cranberries
1 large egg, beaten
1 tbsp milk
4–5 tbsp seedless
   raspberry jam

Preheat the oven to 190°C/375°F/Gas Mark 5, 10 minutes before baking. Lightly oil a large baking sheet.

Sift the flours and baking powder together into a large bowl, then tip in the grains remaining in the sieve.

Cut the butter or margarine into small pieces. It is easier to do this when the butter is in the flour, as it helps stop the butter from sticking to the knife. Rub the butter into the flours until it resembles coarse breadcrumbs. Stir in the sugar and cranberries.

Using a round-bladed knife, stir in the beaten egg and milk. Mix to form a firm dough. Divide the mixture into 12 and roll into balls.

Place the dough balls on the baking sheet, leaving enough space for expansion. Press a thumb into the centre of each ball, making a small hollow. Spoon a little of the jam in each hollow. Brush the tops of the buns lightly with milk.

Bake in the preheated oven for 20–25 minutes until golden brown. Cool on a wire rack and serve.

Try this: FOR AN ALTERNATIVE: 332 FOR A DINNER PARTY: 76

Marbled Chocolate Traybake

MAKES 18 SQUARES

175 g/6 oz butter
175 g/6 oz caster sugar
1 tsp vanilla extract
3 medium eggs,
   lightly beaten

200 g/7 oz self-raising flour
½ tsp baking powder
1 tbsp milk
1½ tbsp cocoa powder

For the chocolate icing:
75 g/3 oz dark chocolate,
   broken into pieces
75 g/3 oz white chocolate,
   broken into pieces

Preheat the oven to 180°C/350°F/Gas Mark 4, 10 minutes before baking. Oil and line a 28 x 18 x 2.5 cm/11 x 7 x 1 inch cake tin with nonstick baking parchment. Cream the butter, sugar and vanilla extract together until light and fluffy. Gradually add the eggs, beating well after each addition. Sift in the flour and baking powder and fold in with the milk.

Spoon half the mixture into the prepared tin, spacing the spoonfuls apart and leaving gaps in between. Blend the cocoa powder to a smooth paste with 2 tablespoons warm water. Stir this into the remaining cake mixture. Drop small spoonfuls between the vanilla cake mixture to fill in all the gaps. Use a knife to swirl the mixtures together a little.

Bake on the centre shelf of the preheated oven for 35 minutes, or until well risen and firm to the touch. Leave in the tin for 5 minutes to cool, then turn out onto a wire rack and leave to cool. Remove the lining.

For the icing, place the plain and white chocolate in separate heatproof bowls and melt each over a saucepan of almost boiling water. Spoon into separate nonstick baking parchment piping bags, snip off the tips and drizzle over the top. Leave to set before serving.

Try this: FOR AN ALTERNATIVE: 330 FOR A DINNER PARTY: 112

Miracle Bars

MAKES 12

100 g/3½ oz butter, melted,
plus 1–2 tsp extra
for oiling
125 g/4 oz digestive
biscuit crumbs
175 g/6 oz chocolate chips

75 g/3 oz shredded or
desiccated coconut
125 g/4 oz chopped
mixed nuts
400 g can sweetened
condensed milk

Preheat the oven to 180°C/350°F/Gas Mark 4, 10 minutes before baking. Generously butter a 23 cm/9 inch square tin and line with nonstick baking parchment.

Pour the butter into the prepared tin and sprinkle the biscuit crumbs over in an even layer.

Add the chocolate chips, coconut and nuts in even layers and drizzle over the condensed milk.

Transfer the tin to the preheated oven and bake for 30 minutes until golden brown.

Allow to cool in the tin, then cut into 12 squares and serve.

Try this: FOR AN ALTERNATIVE: 328 FOR A DINNER PARTY: 54

Chocolate Pecan Traybake

MAKES 12

175 g/6 oz butter
75 g/3 oz icing sugar, sifted
175 g/6 oz plain flour
25 g/1 oz self-raising flour
25 g/1 oz cocoa powder

For the pecan topping:
75 g/3 oz butter
50 g/2 oz light muscovado
   sugar
2 tbsp golden syrup

2 tbsp milk
1 tsp vanilla extract
2 medium eggs, lightly
   beaten
125 g/4 oz pecan halves

Preheat the oven to 180°C/350°F/Gas Mark 4, 10 minutes before baking. Lightly oil and line a 28 x 18 x 2.5 cm/11 x 7 x 1 inch cake tin with nonstick baking parchment. Beat the butter and sugar together until light and fluffy. Sift in the flours and cocoa powder and mix together to form a soft dough.

Press the mixture evenly over the base of the prepared tin. Prick all over with a fork, then bake on the shelf above the centre of the preheated oven for 15 minutes.

Put the butter, sugar, golden syrup, milk and vanilla extract in a small saucepan and heat gently until melted. Remove from the heat and leave to cool for a few minutes, then stir in the eggs and pour over the base. Sprinkle with the nuts.

Bake in the preheated oven for 25 minutes, or until dark golden brown, but still slightly soft. Leave to cool in the tin. When cool, carefully remove from the tin, then cut into 12 squares and serve. Store in an airtight container.

Try this: FOR AN ALTERNATIVE: 342 FOR A DINNER PARTY: 90

Nanaimo Bars

MAKES 15

75 g/3 oz unsalted butter
125 g/4 oz dark chocolate,
   roughly chopped
75 g/3 oz digestive
   biscuits, crushed
75 g/3 oz desiccated coconut
50 g/2 oz chopped mixed nuts

For the filling:
1 medium egg yolk
1 tbsp milk
75 g/3 oz unsalted
   butter, softened
1 tsp vanilla extract
150 g/5 oz icing sugar

For the topping:
125 g/4 oz dark chocolate,
   roughly chopped
2 tsp sunflower oil

Oil and line a 28 x 18 x 2.5 cm/11 x 7 x 1 inch cake tin with nonstick baking parchment. Place the butter and chocolate in a heatproof bowl set over a saucepan of almost boiling water until melted, stirring occasionally. Stir in the crushed biscuits, coconut and nuts into the chocolate mixture and mix well. Spoon into the prepared tin and press down firmly. Chill in the refrigerator for 20 minutes.

For the filling, place the egg yolk and milk in a heatproof bowl set over a saucepan of almost boiling water, making sure the bowl does not touch the water. Whisk for 2–3 minutes. Add the butter and vanilla extract to the bowl and continue whisking until fluffy, then gradually whisk in the icing sugar. Spread over the chilled base, smoothing with the back of a spoon and chill in the refrigerator for a further 30 minutes.

For the topping, place the chocolate and sunflower oil in a heatproof bowl set over a saucepan of almost boiling water. Melt, stirring occasionally, until smooth. Leave to cool slightly, then pour over the filling and tilt the tin, so that the chocolate spreads evenly.

Chill in the refrigerator for about 5 minutes, or until the chocolate topping is just set but not too hard, then mark into 15 bars. Chill again in the refrigerator for 2 hours, then cut into slices and serve.

Try this: FOR AN ALTERNATIVE: 324 FOR A DINNER PARTY: 74

Chocolate Brazil & Polenta Squares

MAKES 9

150 g/5 oz shelled Brazil nuts
150 g/5 oz butter, softened
150 g/5 oz soft light
    brown sugar
2 medium eggs,
    lightly beaten
75 g/3 oz plain flour

25 g/1 oz cocoa powder
¼ tsp ground cinnamon
1 tsp baking powder
pinch salt
5 tbsp milk
65 g/2½ oz instant polenta

Preheat the oven to 180°C/350°F/Gas Mark 4, 10 minutes before baking. Oil and line a deep, 18 cm/7 inch, square tin with nonstick baking parchment. Finely chop 50 g/2 oz of the Brazil nuts and reserve. Roughly chop the remainder. Cream the butter and sugar together until light and fluffy. Gradually add the eggs, beating well after each addition.

Sift the flour, cocoa powder, cinnamon, baking powder and salt into the creamed mixture and gently fold in using a large metal spoon or rubber spatula. Add the milk, polenta and the roughly chopped Brazil nuts. Fold into the mixture.

Turn the mixture into the prepared tin, levelling the surface with the back of the spoon. Sprinkle the reserved 50 g/2 oz finely chopped Brazil nuts over the top. Bake the cake on the centre shelf of the preheated oven for 45–50 minutes until well risen and lightly browned and when a clean skewer inserted into the centre of the cake for a few seconds comes out clean.

Leave the cake in the tin for 10 minutes to cool slightly, then turn out onto a wire rack and leave to cool completely. Cut the cake into 9 equal squares and serve. Store in an airtight container.

Try this: FOR AN ALTERNATIVE: 336   FOR A DINNER PARTY: 44

Lemon & Ginger Buns

MAKES 15

175 g/6 oz butter or
  margarine
350 g/12 oz plain flour
2 tsp baking powder
½ tsp ground ginger
pinch salt

finely grated zest of 1 lemon
175 g/6 oz soft light brown
  sugar
125 g/4 oz sultanas
75 g/3 oz chopped
  mixed peel

25 g/1 oz stem ginger,
  finely chopped
1 medium egg
juice of 1 lemon

Preheat the oven to 220°C/425°F/Gas Mark 7, 15 minutes before baking. Cut the butter or margarine into small pieces and place in a large bowl.

Sift the flour, baking powder, ginger and salt together and add to the butter with the lemon zest. Using the fingertips, rub the butter into the flour and spice mixture until it resembles coarse breadcrumbs.

Stir in the sugar, sultanas, chopped mixed peel and stem ginger.

Add the egg and lemon juice to the mixture, then, using a round-bladed knife, stir well to mix. (The mixture should be quite stiff and just holding together.)

Place heaped tablespoons of the mixture onto a lightly oiled baking tray, making sure that the dollops of mixture are spaced well apart.

Using a fork, rough up the edges of the buns and bake in the preheated oven for 12–15 minutes.

Leave the buns to cool for 5 minutes before transferring to a wire rack to cool, then serve. Otherwise, store the buns in an airtight container and eat within 3–5 days.

Try this: FOR AN ALTERNATIVE: 348   FOR A DINNER PARTY: 110

Marbled Toffee Shortbread

MAKES 12

175 g/6 oz butter
75 g/3 oz caster sugar
175 g/6 oz plain flour
25 g/1 oz cocoa powder
75 g/3 oz fine semolina

For the toffee filling:
50 g/2 oz butter
50 g/2 oz soft light
 brown sugar
397 g can condensed milk

For the chocolate topping:
75 g/3 oz dark chocolate
75 g/3 oz milk chocolate
75 g/3 oz white chocolate

Preheat the oven to 180°C/350°F/Gas Mark 4, 10 minutes before baking. Oil and line a 20.5 cm/8 inch square cake tin with nonstick baking parchment. Cream the butter and sugar together until light and fluffy, then sift in the flour and cocoa powder. Add the semolina and mix together to form a soft dough. Press into the base of the prepared tin. Prick all over with a fork, then bake in the preheated oven for 25 minutes. Leave to cool.

To make the toffee filling, gently heat the butter, sugar and condensed milk together until the sugar has dissolved. Bring to the boil, then simmer for 5 minutes, stirring constantly. Leave for 1 minute, then spread over the shortbread and leave to cool.

For the topping, place the different chocolates in separate heatproof bowls and melt one at a time, set over a saucepan of almost boiling water. Drop spoonfuls of each on top of the toffee and tilt the tin to cover evenly. Swirl with a knife for a marbled effect.

Leave the chocolate to cool. When just set, mark into fingers using a sharp knife. Leave for at least 1 hour to harden before cutting into fingers.

Try this: FOR AN ALTERNATIVE: 322   FOR A DINNER PARTY: 60

Chocolate Nut Brownies

MAKES 16

125 g/4 oz butter
150 g/5 oz firmly packed soft
   light brown sugar
50 g/2 oz dark chocolate,
   roughly chopped
   or broken

2 tbsp smooth peanut butter
2 medium eggs
50 g/2 oz unsalted roasted
   peanuts, finely chopped
100 g/3½ oz self-raising flour

For the topping:
125 g/4 oz dark chocolate,
   roughly chopped
   or broken
50 ml/2 fl oz soured cream

Preheat the oven to 180°C/350°F/Gas Mark 4, 10 minutes before baking. Lightly oil and line a 20.5 cm/8 inch square cake tin with greaseproof paper or baking parchment.

Combine the butter, sugar and chocolate in a small saucepan and heat gently until the sugar and chocolate have melted, stirring constantly. Reserve and cool slightly.

Mix together the peanut butter, eggs and peanuts in a large bowl. Stir in the cooled chocolate mixture. Sift in the flour and fold together with a metal spoon or rubber spatula until combined.

Pour into the prepared tin and bake in the preheated oven for about 30 minutes until just firm. Cool for 5 minutes in the tin before turning out onto a wire rack to cool.

For the topping, melt the chocolate in a heatproof bowl over a saucepan of simmering water, making sure that the base of the bowl does not touch the water.

Cool slightly, then stir in the sour cream until smooth and glossy. Spread over the brownies, refrigerate until set, then cut into squares. Serve the brownies cold.

Try this: FOR AN ALTERNATIVE: 326 FOR A DINNER PARTY: 44

Fruit & Nut Refrigerator Fingers

MAKES 12

14 pink and white
  marshmallows
75 g/3 oz luxury dried
  mixed fruit
25 g/1 oz candied orange
  peel, chopped

75 g/3 oz glacé cherries,
  quartered
75 g/3 oz walnuts, chopped
1 tbsp brandy
175 g/6 oz digestive
  biscuits, crushed

225 g/8 oz dark chocolate
125 g/4 oz unsalted butter
1 tbsp icing sugar, for
  dusting (optional)

Lightly oil and line the base of an 18 cm/7 inch tin with nonstick baking parchment. Using oiled kitchen scissors, snip each marshmallow into four or five pieces over a bowl. Add the dried mixed fruit, orange peel, cherries and walnuts to the bowl. Sprinkle with the brandy and stir together. Add the crushed biscuits and stir until mixed.

Break the chocolate into squares and put in a heatproof bowl with the butter, set over a saucepan of almost boiling water. Stir occasionally until melted, then remove from the heat. Pour the melted chocolate mixture over the dry ingredients and mix together well. Spoon into the prepared tin, pressing down firmly.

Chill in the refrigerator for 15 minutes, then mark into 12 fingers using a sharp knife. Chill in the refrigerator for a further 1 hour, or until set. Turn out of the tin, remove the lining paper and cut into fingers. Dust with icing sugar before serving.

Try this: FOR AN ALTERNATIVE: 346 FOR A DINNER PARTY: 100

Chocolate & Orange Rock Buns

MAKES 12

200 g/7 oz self-raising flour
25 g/1 oz cocoa powder
½ tsp baking powder
125 g/4 oz butter
40 g/1½ oz granulated
   sugar

50 g/2 oz candied pineapple,
   chopped
50 g/2 oz ready-to-eat dried
   apricots, chopped
50 g/2 oz glacé cherries,
   quartered

1 medium egg
finely grated zest of
   ½ orange
1 tbsp orange juice
2 tbsp demerara sugar

Preheat the oven to 200°C/400°F/Gas Mark 6, 15 minutes before baking. Lightly oil two baking sheets, or line them with nonstick baking parchment. Sift the flour, cocoa powder and baking powder into a bowl.

Cut the butter into small squares. Add to the dry ingredients, then, using your hands, rub in until the mixture resembles fine breadcrumbs.

Add the granulated sugar, pineapple, apricots and cherries to the bowl and stir to mix. Lightly beat the egg together with the grated orange zest and juice. Drizzle the egg mixture over the dry ingredients and stir to combine. The mixture should be fairly stiff but not too dry. Add a little more orange juice, if needed.

Using two teaspoons, shape the mixture into 12 rough heaps on the prepared baking sheets. Sprinkle generously with the demerara sugar. Bake in the preheated oven for 15 minutes, switching the baking sheets around after 10 minutes. Leave on the baking sheets for 5 minutes to cool slightly, then transfer to a wire rack to cool. Serve warm or cold.

Try this: FOR AN ALTERNATIVE: 338   FOR A DINNER PARTY: 96

Pecan Caramel Millionaire's Shortbread

SERVES 20

125 g/4 oz butter, softened
2 tbsp smooth peanut butter
75 g/3 oz caster sugar
75 g/3 oz cornflour
175 g/6 oz plain flour

For the topping:
200 g/7 oz caster sugar
125 g/4 oz butter
2 tbsp golden syrup
75 g/3 oz liquid glucose
75 ml/3 fl oz water

400 g can sweetened
condensed milk
175 g/6 oz pecans, roughly
chopped
75 g/3 oz dark chocolate
1 tbsp butter

Preheat the oven to 180°C/350°F/Gas Mark 4, 10 minutes before baking. Lightly oil and line an 18 x 28 cm/7 x 11 inch cake tin with greaseproof paper or baking parchment.

Cream together the butter, peanut butter and sugar until light. Sift in the cornflour and plain flour together and mix in to make a smooth dough. Press the mixture into the prepared tin and prick all over with a fork. Bake in the preheated oven for 20 minutes, until just golden. Remove from the oven.

Meanwhile, for the topping, combine the sugar, butter, golden syrup, glucose, water and condensed milk in a heavy-based saucepan. Stir constantly over a low heat, without boiling, until the sugar has dissolved. Increase the heat, boil steadily, stirring constantly, for about 10 minutes until the mixture turns a golden caramel colour. Remove from the heat and add the pecans. Pour over the shortbread base. Allow to cool, then refrigerate for at least 1 hour.

Break the chocolate into small pieces and put into a heatproof bowl with the butter. Place over a saucepan of barely simmering water, ensuring that the bowl does not come into contact with the water. Leave until melted, then stir together well.

Remove the shortbread from the refrigerator and pour the chocolate evenly over the top, spreading thinly to cover. Leave to set, cut into squares and serve.

Try this: FOR AN ALTERNATIVE: 328   FOR A DINNER PARTY: 90

Triple Chocolate Brownies

MAKES 15

350 g/12 oz dark chocolate, broken into pieces
225 g/8 oz butter, cubed
225 g/8 oz caster sugar
3 large eggs, lightly beaten
1 tsp vanilla extract
2 tbsp very strong black coffee

100 g/3^1/$_2$ oz self-raising flour
125 g/4 oz pecans, roughly chopped
75 g/3 oz white chocolate, roughly chopped
75 g/3 oz milk chocolate, roughly chopped

Preheat the oven to 190°C/375°F/Gas Mark 5, 10 minutes before baking. Oil and line a 28 x 18 x 2.5 cm/11 x 7 x 1 inch cake tin with nonstick baking parchment. Place the plain chocolate in a heatproof bowl with the butter, set over a saucepan of almost boiling water and stir occasionally until melted. Remove from the heat and leave until just cool but not beginning to set.

Place the caster sugar, eggs, vanilla extract and coffee in a large bowl and beat together until smooth. Gradually beat in the chocolate mixture. Sift the flour into the chocolate mixture. Add the pecans and the white and milk chocolate and gently fold in until mixed thoroughly.

Spoon the mixture into the prepared tin and level the surface. Bake on the centre shelf of the preheated oven for 45 minutes, or until just firm to the touch in the centre and crusty on top. Leave to cool in the tin, then turn out onto a wire rack. Trim off the crusty edges and cut into 15 squares.

Try this: FOR AN ALTERNATIVE: 318   FOR A DINNER PARTY: 34

Fruit & Nut Flapjacks

MAKES 12

75 g/3 oz butter or
   margarine
125 g/4 oz soft light
   brown sugar
3 tbsp golden syrup
50 g/2 oz raisins

50 g/2 oz walnuts,
   roughly chopped
175 g/6 oz rolled oats
50 g/2 oz icing sugar
1–1½ tbsp lemon juice

Preheat the oven to 180°C/350°F/Gas Mark 4, 10 minutes before baking. Lightly oil a 23 cm/9 inch square cake tin.

Melt the butter or margarine with the sugar and syrup in a small saucepan over a low heat. Remove from the heat.

Add the raisins, walnuts and oats to the syrup mixture and stir well.

Spoon evenly into the prepared tin and press down well. Transfer to the preheated oven and bake for 20–25 minutes.

Remove from the oven and leave to cool in the tin. Cut into bars while still warm.

Sift the icing sugar into a small bowl, then gradually beat in the lemon juice a little at a time to form a thin icing.

Place into an icing bag fitted with a writing nozzle, then pipe thin lines over the flapjacks. Allow to cool and then serve.

Try this: FOR AN ALTERNATIVE: 338   FOR A DINNER PARTY: 100

Apricot & Almond Slice

SERVES 6

2 tbsp demerara sugar
25 g/1 oz flaked almonds
400 g can apricot halves,
    drained
225 g/8 oz butter

225 g/8 oz caster sugar
4 medium eggs
200 g/7 oz self-raising flour
25 g/1 oz ground almonds
½ tsp almond extract

50 g/2 oz ready-to-eat dried
    apricots, chopped
3 tbsp clear honey
3 tbsp roughly chopped
    almonds, toasted

Preheat the oven to 180°C/350°F/Gas Mark 4, 10 minutes before baking. Oil a 20.5 cm/8 inch square cake tin and line with nonstick baking parchment.

Sprinkle the sugar and the flaked almonds over the parchment, then arrange the apricot halves cut-side down on top.

Cream the butter and sugar together in a large bowl until light and fluffy.

Gradually beat the eggs into the butter mixture, adding a spoonful of flour after each addition of egg. When all the eggs have been added, stir in the remaining flour and the ground almonds and mix thoroughly.

Add the almond extract and the apricots and stir well.

Spoon the mixture into the prepared tin, taking care not to dislodge the apricot halves. Bake in the preheated oven for 1 hour, or until golden and firm to the touch.

Remove from the oven and allow to cool slightly for 15–20 minutes. Turn out carefully, discard the lining paper and transfer to a serving dish. Pour the honey over the top of the cake, sprinkle on the toasted almonds and serve.

Try this: FOR AN ALTERNATIVE: 316   FOR A DINNER PARTY: 76

Index